CONTENTS

INTRODUCTION

The Cricket CoachMaster will show you how to become the complete batsman and batting coach

This manual is designed to be used by: • Teachers • Coaches • Individual players	**It can be used successfully for:** • Group coaching sessions • Individual learning • Coaching of coaches

The Manual contains:

• Step-by-step technical guidance on how to play all the batting shots
• Group coaching activities for the major shots in order of their importance for teaching young players
• Innovative competitive conditioned games to develop cricket awareness
• Notes on attitude and mental preparation (suitable to be used as lecture notes)

This manual is designed to help the development of cricket, by improving standards of teaching, coaching and playing. They will also give you a better overall understanding of the game.

The Group Coaching pages teach SAFETY and ENJOYMENT, through REPETITIONS with MAXIMUM ACTIVITY.

The Game pages teach match tactics and cricket awareness, with additional comments on competitiveness and how to measure improving performance.

Used constructively, this manual will help to improve the skills of a wide range of cricketers, from the professional to the young school player.

WHAT QUALITIES DOES A GOOD COACH NEED TO HAVE?

• GOOD COMMUNICATION
• UNDERSTANDING OF THE GAME
• GOOD TECHNICAL KNOWLEDGE
• LEADERSHIP QUALITIES
• ENTHUSIASM

• GOOD DEMONSTRATION SKILLS
• A GOOD SENSE OF HUMOUR
• A POSITIVE ATTITUDE
• KNOWLEDGE AND UNDERSTANDING OF HIS PLAYERS
• A SMART AND WELL TURNED OUT APPEARANCE

WHAT IS A COACH?

• A TEACHER
• A COMMUNICATOR
• A MANAGER
• A DISCIPLINARIAN
• A MOTIVATOR
• AN ENTHUSIAST
• A TECHNICIAN

BASIC GUIDELINES FOR SUCCESS

TIPS FOR THE PLAYER

- Always be well turned out and on time for practice
- Practise with a purpose and a personal goal
- Practise as if you were playing in a match situation
- Practise good habits
- Focus your concentration while practising
- Be hungry for success — but show good sportsmanship
- Enjoy your practice

Never stop working at your game even when you're at the top.

TIPS FOR THE COACH

(You must be fanatical about safety - it is your number one priority)

- A good coach can correct a complexed problem with a simple solution
- A good coach knows when to change techniques and when to leave alone
- A good coach can spot a problem at the source, rather than later on in a sequence of events
- Fault analysis should always be followed up with positive correction and praise
- When group coaching, work as one coach per ten players
- Always position yourself where you can see everybody, and continually monitor all groups
- Follow group practices with a conditioned game (when possible)
- When coaching batting, always monitor *grip*, *stance* and *backlift* in order to correct technique and improve on bad habits
- Recap *grip*, *stance* and *backlift* when coaching follow-up sessions - they are the source of 80% of batting faults
- Straight-batted shots are *top hand dominant*, with the exception of the flick off the leg and leg glances
- Shots where the bat swings horizontally are all *bottom hand dominant*
- Coaching sessions should be SAFE, hard work and enjoyable
- When running a net session, never have more than six players
- Never leave children unattended with balls: always collect them at break intervals
- Never sacrifice SAFETY for maximum activity
- Encourage the use of helmets in nets and match practice
- Always project your voice with confidence
- Always carry a selection of cricket balls, tennis balls and Incrediballs®/Wind Balls®
- Never mix tennis balls and cricket balls in the same bag: a child may mistakenly take out a hard ball
- Never ask a group of children to throw you a ball: single out just one (otherwise you may be bombarded!)
- Make sure you use the correct size of ball, appropriate to the age of the players:
     13 years and under — 4 3/4 oz, Junior Incrediballs®/Wind Balls®
     14 years and over — 5 1/2 oz, Senior Incrediballs®/Wind Balls®
- Make sure the pitches and nets you use are suitably sized, again appropriate to the age of the players:
     Under 11, 20 yards   Under 12, 21 yards   Under 13, 21 yards   13 and over, 22 yards
- Always look out for potential dangers
- All group practices in this manual should be done under the supervision of a coach or coaches
- Fielding Restrictions - No fielders closer than 11 yards U13, 8 yards U15, in front of the wicket from the striker
- Never ever leave a bowling machine unattended, even with adults

---

GOOD COACHING = ENTHUSIASM + REPETITION + DEVELOPMENT

FOCUSED PRACTICE → CONSISTENCY → SUCCESS → MORE ENJOYMENT OF THE GAME

ALWAYS REMEMBER THE THREE Fs — BE FIRM, FAIR, FUN

DISCIPLINED PLAYERS → DISCIPLINED TEAMS → SUCCESSFUL TEAMS

DEVELOP GOOD TECHNIQUE AND BE A MORE VERSATILE PLAYER — BE A MATCH WINNER!

REMEMBER —

SAFETY + DISCIPLINE + MAXIMUM ACTIVITY + ENJOYMENT + TECHNICAL INPUT ...

... MAKE A GOOD COACHING SESSION

PRINCIPLES OF BATTING

1. Keep the full face of the bat on the line of the ball for as long as possible.

2. Build an innings. Start slowly and go up through the gears, gradually accelerating. Try to build partnerships. Initially score in small targets of 10–20.

3. Early in an innings, leave the balls wide of off stump. Play in a narrow V. Build your attacking shots round a solid defence.

4. Get used to the pace and bounce of the wicket before trying to play more attacking shots. Be patient. Control your eagerness to score too quickly.

5. Familiarise yourself with the bowler's pattern of bowling. (You can begin doing this while waiting to get into bat.)

6. Have a look at new bowlers when there is a bowling change. Get used to them, and be ready to punish their bad balls.

7. Know the match situation and have in mind your personal game plan of how you are going to bat. Always know the team's target. Keep assessing targets.

8. Look to get a new batting partner off the mark. Talk to him to relieve any initial nervousness.

9. Good solid defence when building an innings. Play with soft hands and look for singles.

10. Controlled, calculated stroke play when chasing targets. Don't try to hit the ball too hard. Maintain good technique with attacking shots. Play good cricket shots — Don't slog.

11. Disciplined, focused shot selection throughout innings.

12. Total belief in yourself and your batting. WHY? Because you have practised well and you feel good.

13. FINALLY —TOTAL CONCENTRATION ON THE BALL, while still maintaining an overall view of the game (focused, relaxed).

ATTITUDES

BE PREPARED TO BEAT THE ODDS AND WIN

NEVER SAY DIE — NEVER STOP TRYING UNTIL THE LAST BALL IS BOWLED

THERE IS NO ONE LIKE ME AND THERE IS NO TIME LIKE THE PRESENT

PLAY TO WIN — AND ENJOY IT!

THE IMPORTANCE OF DISCIPLINE

DISCIPLINE MINIMISES MISTAKES

A successful player is a disciplined player

Disciplined players make a disciplined team, and a disciplined team is a successful team

Lack of discipline

1. Lack of discipline shows in poor dress. You play as you look and feel. (Are you interested?)

2. Lack of discipline shows in turning up late, or unprepared. (Are you bothered?)

3. Lack of discipline leads to irrational shots under pressure. (Why don't you stick to the game plan?)

4. Lack of discipline is bad for team morale. (We're bothered but we're not sure you are.)

5. Lack of discipline breeds lack of focus and poor performances. (Let's drop him for someone who is bothered.)

Key areas of discipline

1. How you dress

2. Punctuality

3. Obeying instructions

4. Staying cool under pressure

5. Patience

6. Quality of practice

7. Shot selection

8. Concentration

Practice

Practice minimises failure and breeds success

1. Practise in a disciplined manner, creating pressurised match situations. When you are in a match you will be familiar with the situation and less nervous; therefore you will perform better. CONFIDENT IN PRACTICE → CONFIDENT IN A MATCH.

2. Discipline yourself to regular practice times.

3. Practice with a purpose. A short, focused practice is better than a long drawn out practice with no direction and commitment.

4. FOCUSED CONCENTRATION + DISCIPLINED SHOT SELECTION = CONSISTENCY + CONFIDENCE

SUCCESS

SIDES DO NOT JUST WALK OUT ONTO THE PITCH AND WIN — THEY WORK HARD AND TRY TO MAKE IT HAPPEN

TO BE THE BEST YOU HAVE TO BE CONSISTENT AND PUT IN QUALITY WORK

WHAT IS LENGTH?

HEIGHT OF BOUNCE

Below batsman's knee height

HALF VOLLEY — **A**

Between batsman's knee and thigh height

GOOD LENGTH — **B**

Between batsman's knee and waist height

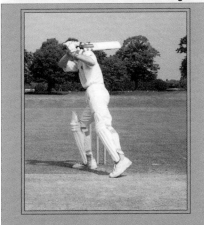

SHORT BALL — **C**

Between batsman's waist and chest height

D

CUT SHOT – Played to a short ball wide of the off stump (fast bowler)

WHAT IS LINE?

This chart shows what shots are best played to the various lengths and lines

OFF STUMP	MIDDLE STUMP	LEG STUMP

SHORT-PITCHED		

SWEEP SHOT – Played against a spin bowler

PULL SHOT – Played to a short ball pitching around leg stump line and bouncing at around waist height, to a spin bowler (a long hop)

HOOK SHOT – Played to a short ball pitching on middle and leg line and bouncing at around chest height, to a fast bowler (a bouncer)

7

TWO METHODS FOR OBTAINING THE CORRECT GRIP AND STANCE

First Method

1. Hold the back of the bat with your right hand (if right-handed batsman).

2. Shake hands with the handle, with your top hand (left hand if right-handed batsman). Top hand V should be half-way between the middle of the back of the bat and the outside edge.

3. Slide your bottom hand up the bat until it meets the top hand. Bottom hand V should be pointing straight down the middle of the back of the bat.

4. With the hands together in the middle of the handle, rest them on the inside thigh of your leading leg (left leg if right-handed batsman). Turn the bat face inwards slightly and rest it against the toes of your back leg. The back of your top hand should point towards mid off.

Second Method

1. Place the bat face down in front of you. The handle should be pointing towards you.

2. Bend down and pick up the bat as if it were an axe. Put your hands in the middle of the handle and make sure they are together.

3. Turn to face the imaginary bowler and imagine you are going to chop down a tree with the full blade of the bat. The Vs of the hands should be in the same position as in the first method.

4. Now rest your hands on the inside thigh of your leading leg and place the bat face up against the toes of your back leg. Turn the bat face in slightly. The back of your top hand should point towards mid off.

THE Vs

The V of the top hand (V formed by the thumb and first finger) should be pointing down the back of the bat, half-way between the middle of the back of the bat and the outside edge. The bottom hand V should be directly in line with the middle of the back of the bat.

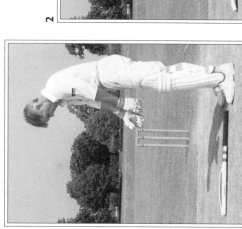

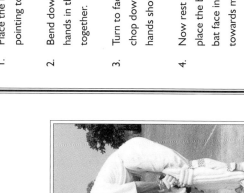

STANCE AND BACKLIFT

When you pick up the bat, keep your head and body position still

Head forward of the body

Eyes level

THINK "RELAXED CONCENTRATION", AND FOCUS ON THE BALL.

Push hands up behind back hip pocket and form diamond shape with arms

Backlift over off stump

TIP – If you want to tap your bat against your back foot as the bowler runs in to bowl, do so. This can give you a rhythm and help your timing.

COACHING POINTS FOR STANCE AND BACKLIFT

1. Stand with one foot either side of the popping crease (about the width of your bat is ideal). The taller you are, the wider apart your feet should be.
2. Your feet should be level and in line with the stumps at the bowler's end.
3. Bend your knees slightly with your weight evenly spread and on the balls of your feet.
4. Your head should be directly above your front foot and forward of your body.
5. Eyes level looking directly up the wicket.
6. Point your head and shoulder directly down the wicket.
7. Rest your hands on the inside thigh of your leading leg with the back of your hand pointing towards mid off.
8. Relax your forearms so they are slightly bent.
9. Rest the face of the bat against the toes of your back foot.
10. Remember: hands together in the middle of the handle.

BACKLIFT

Just as the bowler is about to deliver the ball:

1. Pick up the bat over off stump with a dominant top hand and relaxed bottom hand.
2. Open the bat face slightly.
3. Push your hands up behind your back hip pocket.
4. Bend your leading arm at 90° and free your back arm from your body, thus forming a diamond shape with your arms. (Forearms should be in line with each other.)
5. Hold the handle of the bat loosely with the finger and thumb of the bottom hand – NOT IN THE PALM.

NOW CONCENTRATE AND FOCUS ON THE BALL!

KEEP HEAD AND BODY POSITION STILL DURING BACKLIFT

JUST MOVE THE ARMS TO PICK UP THE BAT

THE FRONT FOOT DRIVES

This is an attacking shot played to a half volley (i.e. a ball that bounces close to the batsman's foot, thus hitting the bat low down, and is easy to hit along the ground).
The Cover Drive is played with exactly the same technique as below, except that the line of the ball is outside off stump and the shot is aimed towards cover.

ON DRIVE

Backlift over off stump
Note – Open leading shoulder slightly, point front foot more

STRAIGHT DRIVE

Backlift over off stump

OFF DRIVE

Backlift over off stump

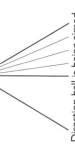

Direction ball is being aimed towards (mid on)

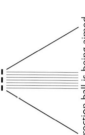

Direction ball is being aimed towards (straight)

Direction ball is being aimed towards (mid off)

BACKLIFT, STEPPING FORWARD TO THE LINE OF THE BALL FOR THE FRONT FOOT DRIVES

As the bowler is about to deliver the ball:

1. With a dominant top hand and relaxed bottom hand, pick up bat over off stump, open bat face slightly.
- Push hands up behind back hip pocket
- Create diamond shape with arms
- Leading elbow bent at 90°, pointing down wicket
- Free rear arm from body
- Bottom hand holds bat with fingers and thumb only

2. From sideways position, lean towards ball with head and shoulder forward of body. Backlift remains raised over off stump.
- Eyes level
- Leave hands behind hip pocket
- Head in line with ball, forward of front foot
- Head and leading shoulder pointing up the wicket

3. Step towards the line of the ball, and bend front knee. Keep back leg straight. (Note differences for on drive.)
- Weight on front foot
- Head directly above front foot
- Inside toe of back foot touching ground
- Maintain sideways position of body

EXECUTING FRONT FOOT DRIVES

Do not try to hit the ball too hard

Think! Let the ball come, and stroke it with correct technique

4. From top of backlift, SWING arms and full face of bat towards line of ball, with forearms passing close to body.
- Arms maintain diamond shape throughout
- Keep arms relaxed at all times
- Top hand controls shot, bottom hand guides bat

5. Strike ball forward of the front foot, keeping top hand dominant and bottom hand relaxed.
- Hands forward of bat face on impact
- Bottom hand – hold bat with fingers and thumb only
- Forearms in line with each other
- Strike ball with full face of bat
- Inside toe of back foot grounded (not tip of toe)

6. Complete follow-through with leading elbow high above hands and close to the head. Toe of bat follows the line of the ball.
- Eyes remain level
- Diamond shape still maintained with arms
- Looking through the hands
- Keep back leg straight
- Bottom hand – hold with fingers and thumb only
- Hands high

HOLD THE SHAPE OF THE SHOT FOR A SECOND OR TWO, BALANCED

LOOK TO DRIVE BALL AS STRAIGHT AS POSSIBLE – THE STRAIGHTEST DRIVES ARE THE SAFEST DRIVES

THE FRONT FOOT DRIVES (INCLUDING ON DRIVE)

OFF AND STRAIGHT DRIVES

ON DRIVE

Note — Shorter stride, dip head and shoulders

Good step technique towards ball, backlift remains raised, head leads body

EXECUTING FRONT FOOT DRIVES

OFF AND STRAIGHT DRIVES

ON DRIVE

Diamond shape formed by the arms (high elbow)

Stand taller for on drive

AIM — TO HIT TOWARDS STRAIGHT MID ON WITH THE FULL FACE OF THE BAT

COACHING POINTS TO LOOK FOR FROM SIDE VIEW

1. Lean towards ball with head and shoulder forward of body.
2. Good step forward towards the pitch of the ball, head directly above the front foot.
3. Backlift remains raised (hands up high behind back hip pocket).
4. Weight on bent front leg.
5. Back leg straight with heel raised and inside of toe touching the floor, thus ensuring sideways body position.
6. Diamond shape maintained by arms throughout shot.
7. Bat swings through the line of the ball.
8. Toe of bat follows direction in which ball has been hit.
9. Leading elbow high, close to head.
10. Bottom hand, fingers and thumb grip (to allow flow of arms and bat through line of ball).
11. High hands above eye level after the ball has been struck, forearms in line with the bat.

DIFFERENCES WITH FRONT FOOT ON DRIVES

Think! Time the ball with correct technique

1. Dip head and shoulder more than for off and straight drives, and LET THE BALL COME MORE.
2. Open leading shoulder to point at straight mid on, so hip opens slightly, allowing the bat to swing through. (Maintain more open body position throughout.)
3. Take a SHORT stride towards the ball, stand tall on balls of feet and point toe of front foot directly up the wicket.
4. Plant front foot down the line of the leg stump — NO WIDER. (If you miss the ball it should hit your front pad.)
5. Stand tall, get up onto toes with weight on front foot and head forward and directly above body. EYES LEVEL.
6. As the bat SWINGS through the line of the ball, work harder to maintain:
   - Dominant top hand
   - Relaxed fingers and thumb bottom hand grip
   - Diamond shape with arms (high leading elbow)
   - High hands
   - Hands forward of bat face on impact

MAKE CONTACT WITH BALL FORWARD AND DIRECTLY IN LINE WITH FRONT LEG

NOTE — Only on leg stump line can this on drive become a FLICK OFF THE LEGS — a low-risk, improvised scoring shot, useful when a fielder is blocking mid on, in one-day cricket.

11

GROUP COACHING FOR THE FRONT FOOT DRIVES

THINK! ENJOYMENT MINIMISES BOREDOM AND ENCOURAGES REPETITION   (REPETITION → DEVELOPMENT)

IMPORTANT OVERALL TIPS FOR THE COACH

SAFETY (MOST IMPORTANT)

1. Use Wind Balls® Incrediballs® or tennis balls. NEVER USE CRICKET BALLS INDOORS WHEN GROUP COACHING. Cricket balls should be used outdoors only, and only with competent players.

2. (a) Always make sure there is a good distance between each group.
   (b) Always make sure each group hits the ball away from each other or into walls.
   (c) Always look for potential dangers. Keep an eye on your suspect players, and position yourself where you can see everybody.
   (d) Don't let fielders stand too close to the batsmen.
   (e) Be strict on safety and punish offenders (i.e. sit-ups, press-ups, etc.); but always have fun.
   (f) Maintain an authoritative voice so that you are always heard.

MOTIVATION

3. (a) Give plenty of praise before constructive criticism.
   (b) Be strict but humorous and always have fun.
   (c) Conclude practice with praise about positive improvement.

COACHING PROGRESSION

4. Always follow practice with a conditioned competitive game of what you have been working on.

SUMMARY OF PRACTICE

5. Recap of coaching points, plus encouragement and praise.

DEMONSTRATION OF SHOT AND PRACTICE WITH GROUP

5 minutes maximum and don't waffle
Project your voice, and be precise and to the point
Coach should always have his bat with him!

The coach explains the front foot drives with players sat in front of him. It is an ATTACKING SHOT played off the front foot. It is used to score runs and hit boundaries. The shot is used more when you have already played yourself in and have runs on the board.

This shot is played to a half volley which bounces near the batsman's front foot and hits the bat low down. This makes it easy to hit it successfully along the ground.

1. Coach executes silent demonstration without the ball, once side on, once front on.

2. Coach executes slow-motion demonstration, once side on, once front on, and introduces one or two coaching points.

3. Coach numbers off groups and sets up first group to show how practice works; others watch. (Put left-handers in the same group, if possible.)

4. Coach takes place of batsman in demonstration group and executes the shot, with the ball, one last time (explaining line, length and bounce of feed).

5. When first group is operational coach goes round and sets up other groups. MONITOR ALL GROUPS AT ALL TIMES — SAFETY.

SET UP FOR THE PRACTICE

1. Set up practice as shown below.
2. Target area: 20 metres away from batsman — SAFETY.
3. Target area: 10–15 metres wide. Fielders stand between markers. NOTE — FOR BETTER PLAYERS TARGET AREA SHOULD BE FURTHER AWAY AND MORE NARROW.
4. Mark out parallel lines on the floor to show line of feed.
5. FOR BETTER PLAYERS TARGET AREA SHOULD BE FURTHER AWAY AND MORE NARROW.
6. Ideal number for groups is 4–6 players — MAXIMUM ACTIVITY.
7. Feeder stands 10–12 paces from batsman.
8. Feeder says "Bat up!", then feeds a BOBBLE FEED, which bounces more than twice below the batsman's knee height. (Underarm feed standing up.)
8. Each group has 3 balls.
9. Ideal duration of practice: 25–35 minutes.

RULES OF THE PRACTICE

1. Each player has 8–10 feeds, then all rotate clockwise.
2. Give groups 2–3 coaching points to work on.
3. Have about 3–4 rounds each (depending on time limit).
4. For the first round of 8–10 play every other shot with the top hand only. (This shows the importance of the top hand.) Play further rounds with two hands.
5. Make the last round competitive: who can hit all balls through target area along the ground? Fielders must stop ball.
6. If players leave the ball they get another feed. If they play and miss they don't.
7. If players deliberately play cross-batted shots on leg side they lose that round. (Be strict on this point — SAFETY.)
8. If players hit the ball into the air, over the fielders, it doesn't count and they lose that feed.
9. On the competitive round, if a player gets out all change round.

DON'T SET UP GROUPS TOO CLOSE TO ONE ANOTHER — THINK SAFETY! COACH POSITIONS HIMSELF WHERE HE CAN MONITOR ALL GROUPS SAFELY

COACHING POINTS (IN ORDER OF IMPORTANCE)

For younger players, introduce one point at a time.

1. High backlift over off stump with dominant top hand. (Bottom hand fingers and thumb grip.)
2. Lean towards ball with head and shoulder (eyes level).
3. Take a good step forward towards the ball. (Weight over front foot.)
4. With dominant top hand and diamond shape formed with arms, SWING bat through the line of the ball. (Forearms passing close to body.)
5. Strike ball forward of front pad, directly below eye level.
6. Keep leading elbow high, throughout the shot.
7. Top hand dominates throughout the shot, bottom hand assists on impact. (Bottom hand fingers and thumb grip.)
8. Finish the shot with high hands, with toe of bat pointing towards target area.
9. Hold position of body for two seconds to show that you are balanced (looking forward through lower forearm).

REMEMBER: TIME THE BALL WITH CORRECT TECHNIQUE — DON'T TRY TO HIT IT TOO HARD

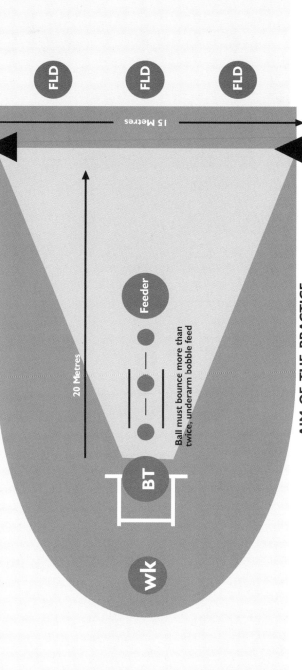

15 Metres

FLD   FLD   FLD

20 Metres

Feeder

BT

wk

Ball must bounce more than twice, underarm bobble feed

AIM OF THE PRACTICE

To drive the ball successfully along the ground in the V towards the target area. This shows you how to play an attacking shot off the front foot and score runs without getting out. THE SAFEST DRIVES ARE THE STRAIGHTEST ONES.

THE FRONT FOOT DRIVING GAME

Now you have learned the front foot drives, try to play the appropriate drives to the various lines of delivery.

TIPS FOR THE COACH

1. **NEVER USE CRICKET BALLS INDOORS**

   USE CRICKET BALLS OUTDOORS ONLY, AND ONLY WITH COMPETENT PLAYERS

2. **SAFETY**

3. **MOTIVATION AND ENCOURAGEMENT**

4. **TEAM SPIRIT**

5. **COMPETITIVENESS**

6. **CLEAR DEMONSTRATIONS**

7. **SUMMARY OF GAME, RECAP COACHING POINTS, AND PRAISE**

LAYOUT FOR THE GAME

(Set up as shown opposite)

1. Mark out creases and boundary areas with cones. If playing inside, use chalk or make use of lines already marked on the floor.

2. Use three sets of stumps.

3. Position incoming batsmen behind the wickets and to the LEG SIDE of the playing area — SAFE FROM INCOMING THROWS AND DRIVES HIT BY THE BATSMAN.

4. Coach stands 15 paces away from the batsman.

5. Set the game up, do a quick demonstration and explain the rules (see opposite).

6. Fielders must be AT LEAST 20 METRES AWAY FROM THE BATSMAN.

7. When playing outside, mark out a wider target area and utilise all the space available. (For better players, put the boundary further away.)

8. Depending on the space available and the distance of the fielders from the batsman, judge the distance a batsman must run to ONLY JUST complete two runs. Mark out this crease with cones. (For younger players, mark a wider target area and have the cones closer.)

RULES OF THE GAME

Play as: TEAMS, 6–8 a side
INDIVIDUALS, 8–10 players

1. Coach feeds: (i) a bobble feed to all players; or (ii) a half volley to better players.

2. All fielders except the wicket keeper and the player backing up MUST stand on the boundary between the cones until the ball is fed. (Coach keeps hold of the ball when feeding every so often, to check whether fielders are moving too early.)

3. Ball must be DRIVEN towards target area, along the ground, and NOT DEFENDED. It must pass the first set of cones or the batsman is out. The batsman MUST complete 2 runs after striking the ball.

4. The ball must be hit in the V to score runs. If it is hit outside that area or behind the wicket the batsman is out. (Give younger players another feed.)

5. The wicket keeper must take incoming throws to the stumps either side of the original ones. OFF SIDE shots must be thrown to stumps on the OFF SIDE — SAFETY. LEG SIDE shots must be thrown to stumps on the LEG SIDE — SAFETY.

6. SCORING (Batsmen bat one at a time):
   - 4 runs if the ball is hit through the target area along the ground.
   - 2 runs if the ball is hit towards the boundary and the batsman completes 2 runs.
   - 2 runs if a fielder stops the ball with his foot.
   - I run if fielders move off the boundary too early.
   - 4 runs if the player backing up the wicket keeper misses the ball (when boundary is not hit).

7. WAYS OF GETTING OUT: Bowled, caught, stumped, run out (no LBW).
   Also: not completing 2 runs after hitting the ball (unless boundary is hit); hitting the ball outside the V; not hitting the ball past the first set of cones; hitting the ball over the fielders on the boundary.

VARIATIONS OF THE GAME

AS TEAMS (6–8 a side)

(A) Each batsman has 6 feeds. If he is out he scores –4. When all the batsmen have batted they switch to fielding. (If time allows, play a second innings.)

(B) Each batsman has 4–6 feeds. If he is out the next batsman comes in. If the batsman isn't out he returns to the back of the queue of waiting batsmen, until it is his turn again. The batting team bat until all the batsmen are out. The last batsman has unlimited feeds. If a batsman hits a 4 another feed is added.

AS INDIVIDUALS (8–10 players)

(A) Each individual bats until he is out. When a batsman is given out, all the fielders move clockwise one round from their previous position.

(B) Each individual batsman has 6–8 feeds. If he is out he scores –4. When a batsman is given out, all the fielders move clockwise one round from their previous position.

ALL OF THE ABOVE VARIATIONS CAN BE PLAYED AS:

(i) Tip and run.

(ii) 2 balls to score or you are out. If you miss a ball it counts as a feed. If you leave the ball you get another feed.

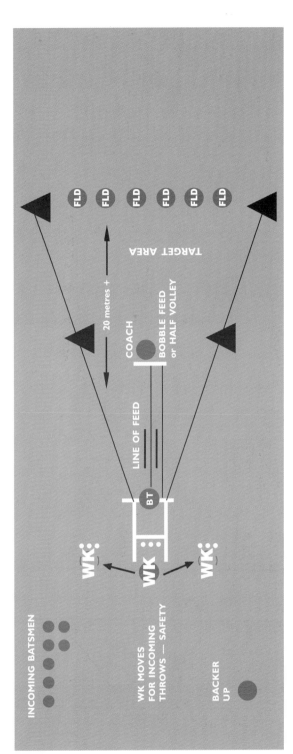

AIM OF THE PRACTICE

To drive the ball successfully along the ground in the V towards the target area. This shows how to play a low-risk attacking shot. The game encourages batsmen to try to run 2 runs when the ball is hit towards the boundary, thus putting pressure on the fielders. This is an important tactic in run–chase situations.

THE FRONT FOOT DEFENCE

This is a defensive shot played to a good length ball pitching in line with the stumps, but not far enough up to drive off the front foot without hitting the ball into the air. You use it more than any other shot, to play yourself in and build an innings. This shot is the foundation of your innings.

Leaning in and stepping forward

Middle and off

Leg stump

Lean with head and shoulder

Pad directly in line with the ball, body position open slightly more on leg stump line

EXECUTING THE SHOT

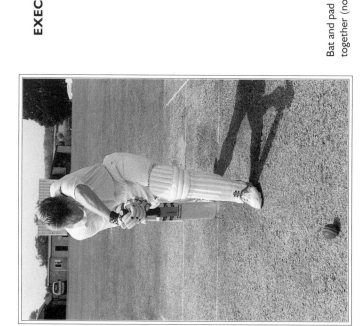

Bat and pad together (no gap)

Looking through hands and high leading elbow on completion of shot

---

BACKLIFT, LEANING IN AND STEPPING FORWARD TO THE LINE OF THE BALL TO PLAY THE FRONT FOOT DEFENCE

As the bowler is about to deliver the ball:

1. With a dominant top hand and relaxed bottom hand, pick up bat over off stump, open bat face slightly.
- Push hands up behind back hip pocket
- Create diamond shape with arms
- Leading elbow bent at 90°, pointing down wicket
- Free rear arm from body
- Bottom hand holds bat with fingers and thumb only

2. From sideways position, lean towards ball, with head and shoulder forward of body. Backlift remains raised over off stump.
- Keep eyes level
- Leave hands up behind hip pocket
- Keep head in line with ball, forward of front foot

3. Step to line of ball, bend front knee, keep back leg straight. (Note difference for leg stump line deliveries.)
- Weight on front foot
- Head directly above front foot
- Inside toe of back leg grounded
- Maintain sideways position of body

EXECUTING THE FRONT FOOT DEFENCE

No follow-through with this shot, just stop the ball

Think! Soft hands

4. From top of backlift, push hands and bat face to line of ball, forearms passing close to body.
- Arms maintain diamond shape throughout
- Relaxed arms
- Top hand controls shot, bottom hand guides bat
- Forearms in line with ball

5. Make contact with ball forward of body and just below eye level with dominant top hand. Bottom hand holds bat with fingers and thumb only, acting as a shock absorber.
- Hands forward of bat face on impact (full face of bat)
- No gap between bat and front pad
- Leading elbow close to head
- Look through hands on impact with ball
- FRONT FOOT — HEAD — HANDS in line with each other
- Defend ball so it stops just in front of you

NEVER PLAY FRONT FOOT DEFENCE TOWARDS THE COVERS AREA — YOU COULD GET CAUGHT IN THE SLIPS

LEAVE IT!

THE FRONT FOOT DEFENCE, INCLUDING FRONT FOOT DEFENCE ON LEG STUMP LINE

Leg stump line

Shorter stride towards the ball, backlift remains raised

Off and middle line

Good stride towards the ball, backlift remains raised

EXECUTING FRONT FOOT DEFENCE

Leg stump line

High leading elbow and diamond shape formed with arms

Off and middle line

Strike ball forward of front pad, fingers and thumb bottom hand grip

NOTE — When playing against a fast bowler you must let the ball come to you. The stride down the wicket will not be shorter than the stride played to a spin bowler. When playing against spin look to take a longer stride and get your foot out to meet the ball more, to smother the spin.

COACHING POINTS TO LOOK FOR FROM SIDE VIEW

1. Lean towards ball with head and shoulder forward of body.

2. Good step forward towards the pitch of the ball.

3. Backlift remains raised (hands up high behind back hip pocket).

4. Weight on bent front leg.

5. Back leg straight with heel raised and inside of toe touching the floor, thus ensuring sideways body position.

6. Diamond shape maintained by arms throughout shot.

7. Hands forward of bat face on impact, below eye level.

8. Complete shot looking over the top of the bat handle, with elbow close to head.

9. Strike ball directly below eye level, forward of front pad.

10. Fingers and thumb bottom hand grip maintained on impact. Bottom hand acts as a shock absorber.

DIFFERENCES WITH FRONT FOOT DEFENCE ON LEG STUMP LINE

1. Dip head and shoulder more than for middle and off line deliveries, and LET THE BALL COME MORE.

2. Open leading shoulder to point at straight mid on, so hip opens slightly, allowing you to push bat towards ball. (Maintain more open body position throughout the shot.)

3. Take a SHORTER stride towards the ball and point front foot directly up the wicket. (Weight on ball of front foot.)

4. Plant front foot down the line of the leg stump — NO WIDER. (If you miss the ball it should hit your front pad.)

5. Keep head forward of front foot and directly above body. EYES LEVEL.

6. As bat is PUSHED towards the line of the ball, work harder to maintain:
   • Dominant top hand
   • Relaxed fingers and thumb bottom hand grip
   • Diamond shape with arms (high leading elbow)
   • Head in line with bat handle, eyes level
   • Full face of the bat

MAKE CONTACT WITH BALL FORWARD AND DIRECTLY IN LINE WITH FRONT LEG

NOTE — Only on leg stump line can this defensive shot become a LEG GLANCE — a low-risk, improvised scoring shot used mainly against fast bowlers and bouncing pitches, in one-day cricket.

15 **AIM — TO DEFEND THE BALL TOWARDS MID ON**

GROUP COACHING FOR THE FRONT FOOT DEFENCE

THINK! ENJOYMENT MINIMISES BOREDOM AND ENCOURAGES REPETITION (REPETITION → DEVELOPMENT)

IMPORTANT OVERALL TIPS FOR THE COACH

SAFETY (MOST IMPORTANT)

1. Use Wind Balls® Incrediball® or tennis balls. NEVER USE CRICKET BALLS INDOORS WHEN GROUP COACHING. Cricket balls should be used outdoors only, and only with competent players.

2. (a) Always make sure there is a good distance between each group.
   (b) Always make sure each group hits the ball away from each other or into walls.
   (c) Always look for potential dangers. Keep an eye on your suspect players, and position yourself where you can see everybody.
   (d) Don't let fielders stand too close to the batsmen.
   (e) Be strict on safety and punish offenders (i.e. sit-ups, press-ups, etc.); but always have fun.
   (f) Maintain an authoritative voice so that you are always heard.

MOTIVATION

3. (a) Give plenty of praise before constructive criticism.
   (b) Be strict but humorous and always have fun.
   (c) Conclude practice with praise about positive improvement.

COACHING PROGRESSION

4. Always follow practice with a conditioned competitive game of what you have been working on.

SUMMARY OF PRACTICE

5. Recap of coaching points, plus encouragement and praise.

DEMONSTRATION OF SHOT AND PRACTICE WITH GROUP

5 minutes maximum and don't waffle
Project your voice, and be precise and to the point
Coach should always have his bat with him!

The coach explains the front foot defence with players sat in front of him. It is a DEFENSIVE SHOT, used to protect your stumps. The shot is used most of all when building an innings and playing yourself in. You will play this shot more than any other shot, so perfect it. This shot is played to a straight, good length delivery (i.e. not far enough up to drive and not short enough to go back to).

1. Coach executes silent demonstration without the ball, once side on, once front on.

2. Coach executes slow-motion demonstration, once side on, once front on, and introduces one or two coaching points.

3. Coach numbers off groups and sets up first group to show how practice works; others watch. (Put left-handers in the same group, if possible.)

4. Coach takes place of batsman in demonstration group and executes the shot, with the ball, one last time (explaining line, length and bounce of feed).

5. When first group is operational coach goes round and sets up other groups. MONITOR ALL GROUPS AT ALL TIMES — SAFETY.

SET UP FOR THE PRACTICE

1. Set up practice as shown below.
2. Markers on the floor for fielders to stand on should be 3 metres from batsman. Be strict on this point — SAFETY.
3. Mark out target area for feeder to aim at for the front foot defence.
4. Ideal number for each group is 4–5 players — MAXIMUM ACTIVITY.
5. Feeder kneels 7–10 paces from batsman.
6. Feeder says "Bat up!", then feeds a DART FEED, bending on one knee, throwing from head height downwards. The ball should be aimed to bounce once and hit the batsman on the front knee.
7. Each group has 3 balls.
8. Ideal duration of practice: 20–30 minutes.

RULES OF THE PRACTICE

1. Each player has 8–10 feeds, then all rotate clockwise.
2. Give groups 2–3 coaching points to work on.
3. Have about 3–4 rounds each (depending on time limit).
4. For the first round of 8–10 play every other shot with the top hand only (to show the importance of the top hand).
5. Make the last round competitive: try to survive all 8–10 feeds without getting out. If you're out, change round. On the practice round, players get another feed if one goes wide. On the competitive round, have 8–10 feeds whether players leave the ball or play and miss.
6. If a player deliberately plays an attacking shot he loses that round of 8–10 feeds. (Be strict on this point — SAFETY.)

DON'T SET UP GROUPS TOO CLOSE TO ONE ANOTHER — THINK SAFETY! COACH POSITIONS HIMSELF WHERE HE CAN MONITOR ALL GROUPS SAFELY

COACHING POINTS (IN ORDER OF IMPORTANCE)

For younger players, introduce one point at a time.

1. High backlift over off stump with dominant top hand. (Bottom hand fingers and thumb grip.)
2. Lean towards ball with head and shoulder (eyes level).
3. Take a good step forward towards the ball. (Weight over front foot.)
4. With dominant top hand and diamond shape formed with arms, PUSH bat towards the ball. (Forearms passing close to body.)
5. Strike ball forward of front pad, directly below eye level.
6. Keep leading elbow high, close to head.
7. Top hand dominates throughout the shot.
8. Bottom hand fingers and thumb grip, acting as shock absorber.
9. Look over the top of the handle on completion of the shot. (Head directly above hands, hands directly above front foot.)

PLAY THE BALL WITH SOFT HANDS, SO IT ROLLS BACK UP THE WICKET

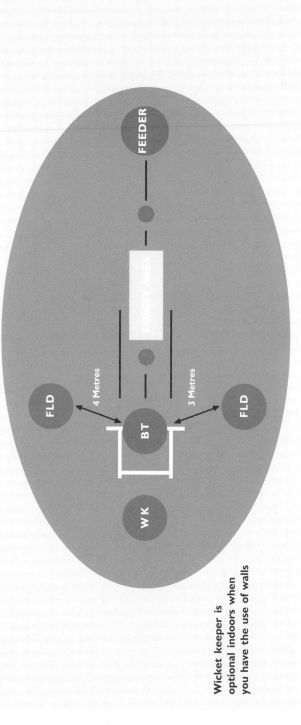

PLAYERS MUST ONLY PLAY DEFENSIVE SHOTS (SAFETY)

Wicket keeper is optional indoors when you have the use of walls

AIM OF THE PRACTICE

To protect the wickets and leave the wide balls; also to defend the ball straight back up the wicket (between the two parallel lines shown above). This is the furthest point away from the close fielders. If you feel you are going to play the ball outside this line on the off side, leave it alone as it is too wide to play at.

16

THE FRONT FOOT DEFENCE SURVIVAL GAME

Now let the players compete, with less emphasis on coaching. This is a game, so have fun with it!

TIPS FOR THE COACH

1. **NEVER USE CRICKET BALLS INDOORS**
   USE CRICKET BALLS OUTDOORS ONLY, AND ONLY WITH COMPETENT PLAYERS
2. **SAFETY**
3. **MOTIVATION AND ENCOURAGEMENT**
4. **TEAM SPIRIT**
5. **COMPETITIVENESS**
6. **CLEAR DEMONSTRATIONS**
7. **SUMMARY OF GAME, RECAP COACHING POINTS, AND PRAISE**

LAYOUT FOR THE GAME

(Set up practice as shown opposite)

1. Play as teams (5–8 a side) or individuals (6–10 players).
2. With chalk or disks, mark out the fielding positions available.
3. Make sure the marks are 3 metres away from the batsman.
4. Short leg must be slightly deeper: 4 metres.
5. Slip or gully in normal position for cricket.
6. Coach must feed when possible (to save arguments).
7. Feed ball as for front foot defence practice (on one knee, 7 or 8 paces away).
8. Encourage fielders to shout "Howzat!" when a catch is taken.
9. Set up the game and do a quick demonstration.
10. Give a batting order.
11. When using more than one team, make it a mini tournament. Winners play winners, losers play losers.

RULES OF THE GAME

1. Every time the batsman survives a delivery he scores a run, even if he leaves the ball. (This teaches him not to play at a wide delivery.)
2. Coach says "Bat up!", then feeds the ball. (Feed as for practice.)
3. The batsman is out if he is:
   (a) bowled, (b) caught, (c) stumped, or (d) if he plays an attacking shot. (Be strict on this last point — SAFETY.) FOR YOUNGER PLAYERS, YOU CAN'T BE OUT FIRST BALL.
4. Fielders must stay on their markers until the ball is hit; if not it is declared a no ball and the batting side scores 2.
5. Nominate a captain and have him position his fielders on the markers appropriate for each incoming batsman (teaching him how to place a field). Always put down more markers than there are fielders.
6. The winner is the team or player that survives the most deliveries.
7. When a player is out all fielders move clockwise to a different position.
8. If the batsmen are too good at this, put the fielders a step or two deeper and play one hand, one bounce.
9. The ideal number for two teams is 8 a side, placed on appropriate markers. The fielders tend to need to be positioned more in front of the wickets for the front foot defence game.
10. Ideal duration of game: 30–40 minutes.

OTHER PROGRESSIONS OF THE GAME

1. USING THE CREASE
   Alternate front foot and back foot defence.
2. JUDGING LENGTH
   Front foot or back foot, feeds at random.
3. For competent players, throw the ball harder.

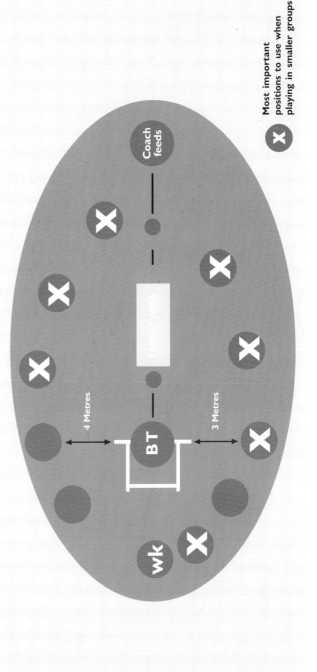

PLAYERS MUST ONLY PLAY DEFENSIVE SHOTS OR THEY ARE OUT (SAFETY)

AIM OF THE GAME

To see which team or individual survives the most deliveries. This simulates playing out for a draw and saving a game.

Most important positions to use when playing in smaller groups

THE BACK FOOT DRIVES

This is an attacking shot played to a short pitched delivery bouncing between the batsman's knee and waist height. The Cover Drive is played with exactly the same technique as below, except that the line of the ball is outside off stump and the shot is aimed towards cover.

OFF DRIVE

STRAIGHT DRIVE

ON DRIVE

Backlift over off stump

Direction ball is being aimed towards (mid off)

Backlift over off stump

Direction ball is being aimed towards (straight)

Backlift over off stump

Note — Open leading shoulder slightly

Direction ball is being aimed towards (mid on)

BACKLIFT, STEPPING BACK AND ACROSS IN LINE TO PLAY THE BACK FOOT DRIVES

As the bowler is about to deliver the ball:

1. With a dominant top hand and relaxed bottom hand, pick up bat over off stump, open bat face slightly.
- Push hands up behind back hip pocket
- Create diamond shape with arms
- Leading elbow bent at 90°, pointing down wicket
- Free rear arm from body
- Bottom hand holds bat with fingers and thumb only

2. From sideways position, dip head and shoulder towards ball. Push off front leg, step back and across crease. Maintain backlift.
- Eyes level, head and body behind line of ball
- Head still forward of body
- Head and shoulder pointing down wicket

3. Plant back foot parallel to crease and maintain sideways position. Weight now on back foot, head over front foot. Front leg slides towards back foot, to act as counterbalance. (Note difference for leg stump line deliveries.)
- Stand tall
- Head forward of body
- Head and shoulder pointing down wicket
- All three stumps should never be showing!
- Toes of front foot resting lightly on the ground

EXECUTING BACK FOOT DRIVES

Do not try to hit the ball too hard

Think! Let the ball come, and stroke it with correct technique

4. From top of backlift, SWING arms and face of bat towards line of ball, with forearms passing close to body.
- Arms maintain diamond shape throughout
- Keep arms relaxed at all times
- Top hand controls shot, bottom hand guides bat

5. Strike ball forward of body below eye level, keeping top hand dominant and bottom hand relaxed.
- Hands forward of bat face on impact
- Bottom hand – hold bat with fingers and thumb only
- Forearms in line with each other
- Strike ball with full face of bat

6. Complete follow-through with leading elbow high above hands and close to head. Toe of bat follows line of the ball.
- Head forward of body
- Eyes remain level
- Diamond shape still maintained with arms
- Leading elbow close to head
- Look through hands
- Bottom hand – hold with fingers and thumb only

HOLD THE SHAPE OF THE SHOT FOR A SECOND OR TWO, BALANCED

LOOK TO DRIVE BALL AS STRAIGHT AS POSSIBLE – THE STRAIGHTEST DRIVES ARE THE SAFEST DRIVES

THE BACK FOOT DRIVES (INCLUDING ON DRIVE)

COACHING POINTS TO LOOK FOR FROM SIDE VIEW

OFF AND STRAIGHT DRIVES

ON DRIVE

Note — More open body position

1. Deep step back and across into crease.
2. Back foot parallel to crease.
   (Note differences for on drives below.)
3. Weight on back foot with head forward of body.
4. Hands up behind back pocket, backlift still raised.
5. Diamond shape maintained with forearms throughout shot.
6. Front leg slides towards back leg with heel raised and toes lightly touching ground (counterbalance).
7. Stand tall, make contact with ball below eye level, forward of body.
8. Bottom hand – fingers and thumb grip (to allow flow of arms and bat through line of ball).
9. Complete the shot with toe of bat following line of ball, keeping leading elbow high and close to head.

Weight on back foot, head stays forward of body

EXECUTING BACK FOOT DRIVES

OFF AND STRAIGHT DRIVES

Back foot parallel to the crease

DIFFERENCES WITH BACK FOOT ON DRIVES

Think! Time the ball with correct technique

1. Dip leading shoulder more and open it slightly, and maintain its position as you step back and across to execute the shot.
2. Step INSIDE the line of the ball, giving you the option of playing the FLICK OFF THE LEGS. (Back leg covers middle and off stump.)
3. Plant back foot tilted slightly inwards towards the covers area to adopt a more open body position.
4. Open hips and front leg towards leg side, allowing you to swing the bat through the line of the ball.
5. As the bat SWINGS through the line of the ball, work harder to maintain:
   • Dominant top hand
   • Relaxed fingers and thumb bottom hand grip
   • Diamond shape with arms
   • High leading elbow position
   • High hands

NOTE — Only on leg stump line can this on drive become a FLICK OFF THE LEGS — a low-risk, improvised scoring shot, useful when a fielder is blocking mid on, in one-day cricket.

ON DRIVE

Back foot turns in slightly, opening position of front leg

AIM — TO HIT THE BALL TOWARDS STRAIGHT MID ON WITH THE FULL FACE OF THE BAT

GROUP COACHING FOR THE BACK FOOT DRIVES

THINK! ENJOYMENT MINIMISES BOREDOM AND ENCOURAGES REPETITION (REPETITION → DEVELOPMENT)

At first, teach the back foot off and straight drives only, to encourage straight-batted shots. These drives should be mastered before the on drive is introduced.

IMPORTANT OVERALL TIPS FOR THE COACH

SAFETY (MOST IMPORTANT)

1. Use Wind Balls®, Incrediballs® or tennis balls. NEVER USE CRICKET BALLS INDOORS WHEN GROUP COACHING. Cricket balls should be used outdoors only, and only with competent players.

2. (a) Always make sure there is a good distance between each group.

   (b) Always make sure each group hits the ball away from each other or into walls.

   (c) Always look for potential dangers. Keep an eye on your suspect players, and position yourself where you can see everybody.

   (d) Don't let fielders stand too close to the batsmen.

   (e) Be strict on safety and punish offenders (i.e. sit-ups, press-ups, etc.); but always have fun.

   (f) Maintain an authoritative voice so that you are always heard.

MOTIVATION

3. (a) Give plenty of praise before constructive criticism.

   (b) Be strict but humorous and always have fun.

   (c) Conclude practice with praise about positive improvement.

COACHING PROGRESSION

4. Always follow practice with a conditioned competitive game of what you have been working on.

SUMMARY OF PRACTICE

5. Recap of coaching points, plus encouragement and praise.

DEMONSTRATION OF SHOT AND PRACTICE WITH GROUP

5 minutes maximum and don't waffle
Project your voice, and be precise and to the point
Coach should always have his bat with him!

The coach explains the back foot drives with players sat in front of him. It is an ATTACKING SHOT played off the back foot. It is used to score runs and hit boundaries. The shot is used more when you have already played yourself in and have runs on the board.

This shot is most frequently played against fast bowling. It is played to a short-pitched ball bouncing between the batsman's knee and waist height, making it easy to get over and hit successfully along the ground.

1. Coach executes silent demonstration without the ball, once side on, once front on.

2. Coach executes slow-motion demonstration, once side on, once front on, and introduces one or two coaching points.

3. Coach numbers off groups and sets up first group to show how practice works; others watch. (Put left-handers in the same group, if possible.)

4. Coach takes place of batsman in demonstration group and executes the shot, with the ball, one last time (explaining line, length and bounce of feed.)

5. When first group is operational coach goes round and sets up other groups. MONITOR ALL GROUPS AT ALL TIMES — SAFETY.

SET UP FOR THE PRACTICE

1. Set up practice as shown below.
2. Target area: 20 metres away from batsman — SAFETY.
3. Target area: 10–15 metres wide. Fielders stand between markers.
4. NOTE — FOR BETTER PLAYERS TARGET AREA SHOULD BE FURTHER AWAY AND MORE NARROW.
5. Mark out parallel lines on the floor to show line and length of feed.
6. Ideal number for groups is 4–6 players — MAXIMUM ACTIVITY.
7. Feeder kneels on one knee, 10–12 paces from the batsman.
8. Feeder says "Bat up!", then feeds a DART FEED which bounces between the batsman's knee and waist height. (Throw from head height downwards, one bounce.)

RULES OF THE PRACTICE

1. All shots to be executed with TWO HANDS (top hand dominant).
2. Each player has 8–10 feeds, then all rotate clockwise.
3. Give groups 2–3 coaching points to work on.
4. Have about 3–4 rounds each (depending on time limit).
5. Make the last round competitive: see who can hit all balls through the target area along the ground. Fielders must stop the ball.
6. If players leave the ball they get another feed. If they play and miss they don't.
7. If players deliberately play cross-batted shots on leg side they lose that round. (Be strict on this point — SAFETY.)
8. If players hit the ball into the air, over the fielders, it doesn't count and they lose that feed.
9. On the competitive round, if a player gets out all change round.

DON'T SET UP GROUPS TOO CLOSE TO ONE ANOTHER — THINK SAFETY! COACH POSITIONS HIMSELF WHERE HE CAN MONITOR ALL GROUPS SAFELY

COACHING POINTS (IN ORDER OF IMPORTANCE)

For younger players, introduce one point at a time.

1. High backlift over off stump with dominant top hand. (Bottom hand fingers and thumb grip.)

2. Step back and across the crease, getting head and body into line with the ball (eyes level).

3. Weight on back foot, which lands parallel to crease (head left forward of the body).

4. With dominant top hand and diamond shape formed with arms, SWING bat through the line of the ball. (Forearms passing close to body.)

5. Strike ball forward of body, directly below eye level.

6. Keep leading elbow high, throughout the shot.

7. Top hand dominates throughout the shot, bottom hand assists on impact. (Bottom hand fingers and thumb grip.)

8. Finish the shot with high hands, with toe of bat pointing towards target area.

9. Hold position of body for two seconds to show that you are balanced (looking through lower forearm).

REMEMBER: TIME THE BALL WITH CORRECT TECHNIQUE — DON'T TRY TO HIT IT TOO HARD

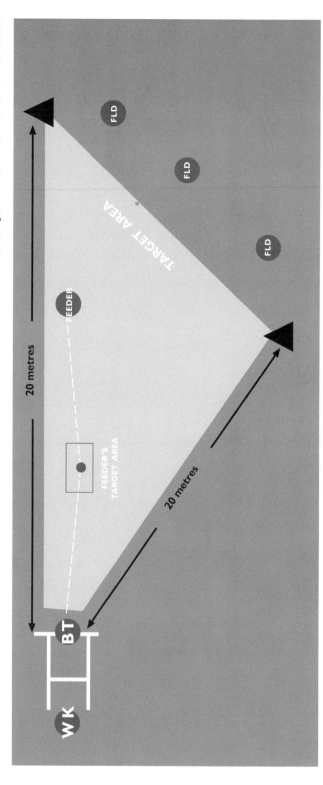

AIM OF THE PRACTICE

To drive the ball successfully along the ground into the target area. This shows you how to play an attacking shot off the back foot and score runs without getting out. THE SAFEST DRIVES ARE THE STRAIGHTEST ONES.

THE BACK FOOT DRIVING GAME

To encourage straight-batted shots, play this game on the off side only with younger players. With competent players, set up the targets to include mid on.

TIPS FOR THE COACH

1. NEVER USE CRICKET BALLS INDOORS

USE CRICKET BALLS OUTDOORS ONLY, AND ONLY WITH COMPETENT PLAYERS

2. SAFETY

3. MOTIVATION AND ENCOURAGEMENT

4. TEAM SPIRIT

5. COMPETITIVENESS

6. CLEAR DEMONSTRATIONS

7. SUMMARY OF GAME, RECAP COACHING POINTS, AND PRAISE

LAYOUT FOR THE GAME

(Set up as shown opposite)

1. Mark out creases and boundary areas with cones. If playing inside, use chalk or make use of lines already marked on the floor.

2. Use three sets of stumps.

3. Position incoming batsmen behind the wickets and to the OFF SIDE of the playing area — SAFE FROM INCOMING THROWS AND DRIVES HIT BY THE BATSMAN.

4. Coach stands 15 paces away from the batsman.

5. Set the game up, do a quick demonstration and explain the rules (see opposite).

6. Fielders must be AT LEAST 15 METRES AWAY FROM THE BATSMAN.

7. When playing outside, mark out a wider target area and utilise all the space available. (For better players, put the boundary further away.)

8. Depending on the space available and the distance of the fielders from the batsman, judge the distance a batsman must run to ONLY JUST complete two runs. Mark out this crease with cones. (For younger players, mark a wider target area and have the cones closer.)

RULES OF THE GAME

Play as: TEAMS, 6–8 a side
 INDIVIDUALS, 8–10 players

1. Coach feeds a dart feed, on one knee.

2. All fielders except the wicket keeper and the player backing up MUST stand on the boundary between the cones until the ball is fed. (Coach keeps hold of the ball when feeding every so often, to check whether fielders are moving too early.)

3. Ball must be DRIVEN towards target area, along the ground, and NOT DEFENDED. It must pass the first set of cones or the batsman is out. The batsman MUST complete 2 runs after striking the ball.

4. The ball must be hit in the V to score runs. If it is hit outside that area or behind the wicket the batsman is out. (Give younger players another feed.)

5. The wicket keeper must take incoming throws to the stumps either side of the original ones. OFF SIDE shots must be thrown to stumps on the OFF SIDE — SAFETY. LEG SIDE shots must be thrown to stumps on the LEG SIDE — SAFETY.

6. SCORING (Batsmen bat one at a time):
 4 runs if the ball is hit through the target area along the ground.
 2 runs if the ball is hit towards the boundary and the batsman completes 2 runs.
 2 runs if a fielder stops the ball with his foot.
 1 run if fielders move off the boundary too early.
 4 runs if the player backing up the wicket keeper misses the ball.

7. WAYS OF GETTING OUT: Bowled, caught, stumped, run out (no LBW).
 Also: not completing 2 runs after hitting the ball (unless boundary is hit); hitting the ball outside the V; hitting the ball over the fielders on the boundary; not hitting the ball past the first set of cones; hitting the ball on the boundary.

VARIATIONS OF THE GAME

AS TEAMS (6 a side)

(A) Each batsman has 6 feeds. If he is out he scores –4. When all the batsmen have batted they switch to fielding. (If time allows, play a second innings.)

(B) Each batsman has 4–6 feeds. If he is out the next batsman comes in. If the batsman isn't out he returns to the back of the queue of waiting batsmen, until it is his turn again. The batting team bat until all the batsmen are out. The last batsman has unlimited feeds. If a batsman hits a 4 another feed is added.

AS INDIVIDUALS (8–10 players)

(A) Each individual bats until he is out. When a batsman is given out, all the fielders move clockwise one round from their previous position.

(B) Each individual batsman has 6–8 feeds. If he is out he scores –4. When a batsman is given out, all the fielders move clock-wise one round from their previous position.

ALL OF THE ABOVE VARIATIONS CAN BE PLAYED AS:

(i) Tip and run.

(ii) 2 balls to score or you are out. If you miss a ball it counts as a feed. If you leave the ball you get another feed.

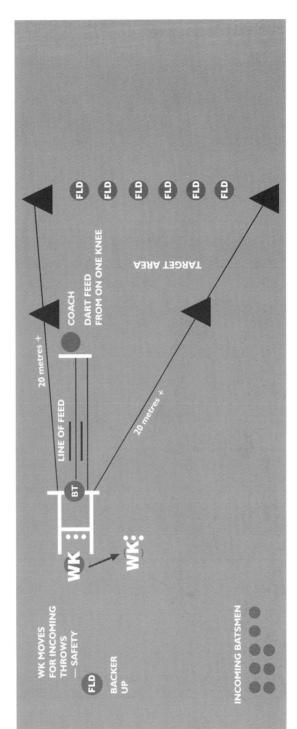

AIM OF THE PRACTICE

To drive the ball off the back foot successfully along the ground between mid off and extra cover. This shows how to play a low-risk attacking shot. The game encourages batsmen to try to run 2 runs when the ball is hit towards the boundary, thus putting pressure on the fielders. This is an important tactic in run–chase situations.

THE BACK FOOT DEFENCE

This is a defensive shot played to a short ball pitching in line with the stumps bouncing between the batsman's waist and chest height. It is played against fast bowlers more frequently than spinners. It plays a large part in building an innings and playing yourself in, especially against fast bowling.

Back foot parallel to the crease

Back foot turns in slightly to adopt more open body position

BACK LEG SHOULD BE COVERING MIDDLE AND LEG STUMP

Back foot parallel to the crease

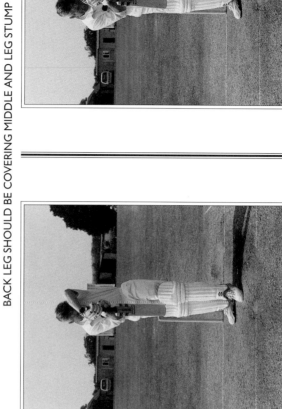

Bat in line with body

Look through hands with high elbows

Front pad opens out slightly towards leg side

NOTE — If ball bounces above chest height, rise up onto toes and slide top hand around back of bat, so you can get your hands and bat higher to play the ball down.

BACKLIFT, STEPPING BACK AND ACROSS INTO LINE TO PLAY THE BACK FOOT DEFENCE

As the bowler is about to deliver the ball:

1. With a dominant top hand and relaxed bottom hand, pick up bat over off stump, open bat face slightly.
- Lift bottom hand up behind back hip pocket
- Create diamond shape with arms
- Leading elbow bent at 90°, pointing down wicket
- Free rear arm from body
- Bottom hand holds bat with fingers and thumb only

2. From sideways position, dip head and shoulder towards ball. Push off front leg, step back and across crease, with backlift still raised over the stumps. (GET HEAD AND BODY IN LINE WITH THE BALL.)
- Keep eyes level
- Keep head forward of body
- Head and leading shoulder pointing down wicket

3. Plant back foot parallel to crease and maintain sideways position. Weight now on back foot, head over front foot. Front leg slides towards back foot, to act as counterbalance. (Note difference for leg stump line deliveries.)
- Stand tall
- Head forward of body
- Head and shoulder pointing down wicket
- All three stumps should never be showing!
- Toes of front foot resting lightly on the ground

EXECUTING THE BACK FOOT DEFENCE

No follow-through with this shot, just stop the ball

Think! Soft hands

4. From top of backlift, push hands and bat face towards ball, forearms passing close to body.
- Arms maintain diamond shape throughout
- Relaxed arms
- Top hand controls shot, bottom hand guides bat
- Forearms in line with ball

5. Make contact with ball forward of body and just below eye level with dominant top hand. Bottom hand holds bat with fingers and thumb only, acting as a shock absorber.
- Hands forward of bat face on impact (full face of bat)
- Leading elbow close to head
- No gap between bat and body
- Look through hands on impact with ball
- BACKFOOT — HEAD — HANDS in line with each other
- Defend ball so it stops just in front of you

NEVER PLAY BACK FOOT DEFENCE TOWARDS THE COVERS AREA — YOU COULD GET CAUGHT IN THE SLIPS

LEAVE IT!

THE BACK FOOT DEFENCE, INCLUDING BACK FOOT DEFENCE ON LEG STUMP LINE

Leg stump line

Dip and open front shoulder more on leg stump line deliveries

Off and straight line

Weight on the back foot, head stays forward of the body

EXECUTING BACK FOOT DEFENCE

Back foot turns in slightly, thus opening position of front leg

Back foot parallel, diamond shape with arms

AIM — TO DEFEND THE BALL TOWARDS STRAIGHT MID ON WITH THE FULL FACE OF THE BAT

COACHING POINTS TO LOOK FOR FROM SIDE VIEW

1. Deep step back into the crease.
2. Back foot parallel to the crease. (Note difference for leg stump line deliveries.)
3. Weight on back foot, head forward of body.
4. Hands up behind back hip pocket, backlift still raised.
5. Diamond shape maintained with forearms throughout shot.
6. Front leg slides towards back leg with heel raised and toes lightly touching ground (counterbalance).
7. Stand tall and make contact with ball below eye level and forward of body.
8. Bottom hand fingers and thumb grip, acting as a shock absorber.
9. Hands forward of bat face on impact with ball.
10. Complete shot looking through hands with high elbow position close to head.

DIFFERENCES WITH BACK FOOT DEFENCE ON LEG STUMP LINE

1. Dip leading shoulder more and open it slightly, and maintain its position as you step back and across to execute the shot.
2. Step INSIDE the line of the ball, giving you the option of playing a LEG GLANCE.
3. Plant back foot tilted slightly inwards towards the covers area to adopt a more open body position. (Back leg covers middle and off stump.)
4. Open hips and front leg towards the leg side, allowing you to PUSH the bat at the ball.
5. As you push the bat towards the line of the ball, work harder to maintain:
   - Dominant top hand
   - Relaxed fingers and thumb bottom hand grip
   - Diamond shape with arms
   - High leading elbow, close to head
   - Full face of bat

NOTE — Only on leg stump line can this defensive shot become a LEG GLANCE — a low-risk, improvised scoring shot, useful in run–chase situations.

GROUP COACHING FOR THE BACK FOOT DEFENCE

THINK! ENJOYMENT MINIMISES BOREDOM AND ENCOURAGES REPETITION (REPETITION → DEVELOPMENT)

IMPORTANT OVERALL TIPS FOR THE COACH

SAFETY (MOST IMPORTANT)

1. Use Wind Balls®, Incrediballs® or tennis balls. NEVER USE CRICKET BALLS INDOORS WHEN GROUP COACHING. Cricket balls should be used outdoors only, and only with competent players.

2. (a) Always make sure there is a good distance between each group.
   (b) Always make sure each group hits the ball away from each other or into walls.
   (c) Always look for potential dangers. Keep an eye on your suspect players, and position yourself where you can see everybody.
   (d) Don't let fielders stand too close to the batsmen.
   (e) Be strict on safety and punish offenders (i.e. sit-ups, press-ups, etc.); but always have fun.
   (f) Maintain an authoritative voice so that you are always heard.

MOTIVATION

3. (a) Give plenty of praise before constructive criticism.
   (b) Be strict but humorous and always have fun.
   (c) Conclude practice with praise about positive improvement.

COACHING PROGRESSION

4. Always follow practice with a conditioned competitive game of what you have been working on.

SUMMARY OF PRACTICE

5. Recap of coaching points, plus encouragement and praise.

DEMONSTRATION OF SHOT AND PRACTICE WITH GROUP

5 minutes maximum and don't waffle
Project your voice, and be precise and to the point
Coach should always have his bat with him!

The coach explains the back foot defence with players sat in front of him. It is a DEFENSIVE SHOT, used to protect your stumps. The shot is used most of all when building an innings and playing yourself in. You will play it more than any other shot, so perfect it. This shot is played to a straight, short-pitched ball too short to go forward to and drive or defend off the front foot.

1. Coach executes silent demonstration without the ball, once side on, once front on.

2. Coach executes slow-motion demonstration, once side on, once front on, and introduces one or two coaching points.

3. Coach numbers off groups and sets up first group to show how practice works; others watch. (Put left-handers in the same group, if possible.)

4. Coach takes place of batsman in demonstration group and executes the shot, with the ball, one last time (explaining line, length and bounce of feed.)

5. When first group is operational coach goes round and sets up other groups. MONITOR ALL GROUPS AT ALL TIMES — SAFETY.

COACHING POINTS (IN ORDER OF IMPORTANCE)

For younger players, introduce one point at a time.

1. High backlift over off stump with dominant top hand. (Bottom hand fingers and thumb grip.)

2. Step back and across the crease, getting head and body into line with the ball (eyes level).

3. Weight on back foot, which lands parallel to crease (head left forward of the body).

4. With dominant top hand and diamond shape formed with arms, PUSH bat towards the ball. (Forearms passing close to body.)

5. Strike ball forward of body, directly below eye level.

6. Keep leading elbow high, close to head.

7. Bottom hand fingers and thumb grip, acting as shock absorber.

8. Top hand dominates throughout the shot.

9. Look THROUGH the handle of the bat on completion of the shot. (Head directly above hands, and in line with back foot.)

PLAY THE BALL WITH SOFT HANDS, SO IT ROLLS BACK UP THE WICKET

SET UP FOR THE PRACTICE

1. Set up practice as shown below.

2. Markers on the floor for fielders to stand on should be 3 metres from batsman (4m for leg side fielder). Be strict on this point — SAFETY.

3. Mark out target area for feeder to aim at for the back foot defence.

4. Ideal number for each group is 4–5 players — MAXIMUM ACTIVITY.

5. Feeder kneels 7–10 paces from batsman.

6. Feeder says "Bat up!", then feeds a DART FEED, standing up, throwing from head height downwards. The ball should be aimed to bounce once and between the batsman's waist and chest height.

7. Each group has 3 balls.

8. Ideal duration of practice: 20–30 minutes.

RULES OF THE PRACTICE

1. Each player has 8–10 feeds, then all rotate clockwise.

2. Give groups 2–3 coaching points to work on.

3. Have about 3–4 rounds each (depending on time limit).

4. For the first round of 8–10 play every other shot with the top hand only (to show the importance of the top hand).

5. Make the last round competitive: try to survive all 8–10 feeds without getting out. If you're out, change round.

6. On the competitive round, players get another feed if one goes wide. On the practice round, have 8–10 feeds whether players leave the ball or play and miss.

7. If a player deliberately plays an attacking shot he loses that round of 8–10 feeds. (Be strict on this point — SAFETY.)

DON'T SET UP GROUPS TOO CLOSE TO ONE ANOTHER — THINK SAFETY!
COACH POSITIONS HIMSELF WHERE HE CAN MONITOR ALL GROUPS SAFELY

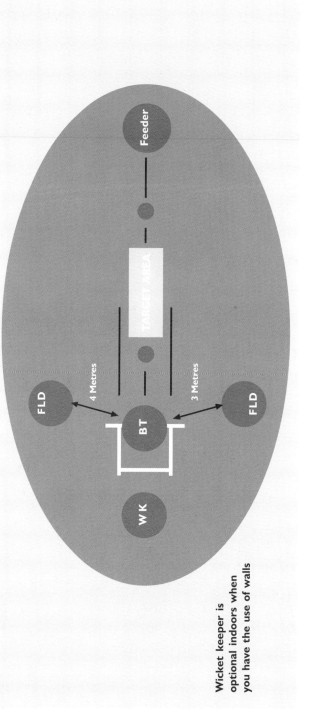

PLAYERS MUST ONLY PLAY DEFENSIVE SHOTS (SAFETY)

Wicket keeper is optional indoors when you have the use of walls

AIM OF THE PRACTICE

To protect the wickets and leave the wide balls; also to defend the ball straight back up the wicket (between the two parallel lines shown above). This is the furthest point away from the close fielders. If you feel you are going to play the ball outside this line on the off side, leave it alone as it is too wide to play at.

THE BACK FOOT DEFENCE SURVIVAL GAME

Now let the players compete, with less emphasis on coaching. This is a game, so have fun with it!

TIPS FOR THE COACH

1. **NEVER USE CRICKET BALLS INDOORS**

   USE CRICKET BALLS OUTDOORS ONLY, AND ONLY WITH COMPETENT PLAYERS

2. **SAFETY**

3. **MOTIVATION AND ENCOURAGEMENT**

4. **TEAM SPIRIT**

5. **COMPETITIVENESS**

6. **CLEAR DEMONSTRATIONS**

7. **SUMMARY OF GAME, RECAP COACHING POINTS, AND PRAISE**

LAYOUT FOR THE GAME

(Set up practice as shown opposite)

1. Play as teams (5–8 a side) or individuals (5–10 players).

2. With chalk or disks, mark out the fielding positions available.

3. Make sure the marks are 3 metres away from the batsman.

4. Short leg must be slightly deeper: 4 metres.

5. Slip or gully in normal position for cricket.

6. Coach must feed when possible (to save arguments).

7. Feed ball as for back foot defence practice (on one knee, 7 or 8 paces away).

8. Encourage fielders to shout "Howzat!" when a catch is taken.

9. Set up the game and do a quick demonstration.

10. Give a batting order.

11. When using more than one team, make it a mini tournament. Winners play winners, losers play losers.

RULES OF THE GAME

1. Every time the batsman survives a delivery he scores a run, even if he leaves the ball. (This teaches him not to play at a wide delivery.)

2. Coach says "Bat up!", then feeds the ball. (Feed as for practice.)

3. The batsman is out if he is:
   (a) bowled, (b) caught, (c) stumped, or
   (d) if he plays an attacking shot. (Be strict on this last point — SAFETY.)
   FOR YOUNGER PLAYERS, YOU CAN'T BE OUT FIRST BALL.

4. Fielders must stay on their markers until the ball is hit; if not it is declared a no ball and the batting side scores 2.

5. Nominate a captain and have him position his fielders on the markers appropriate for each incoming batsman (teaching him how to place a field). Always put down more markers than there are fielders.

6. The winner is the team or player that survives the most deliveries.

7. When a player is out all fielders move clockwise to a different position.

8. If the batsmen are too good at this, put the fielders a step or two deeper and play one hand, one bounce.

9. The ideal number for two teams is 8 a side, placed on appropriate markers. The fielders tend to need to be positioned more in front of the wickets for the back foot defence game.

10. Ideal duration of game: 30–40 minutes.

OTHER PROGRESSIONS OF THE GAME

1. **USING THE CREASE**
   Alternate front foot and back foot defence.

2. **JUDGING LENGTH**
   Front foot or back foot, feeds at random.

3. For competent players, throw the ball harder.

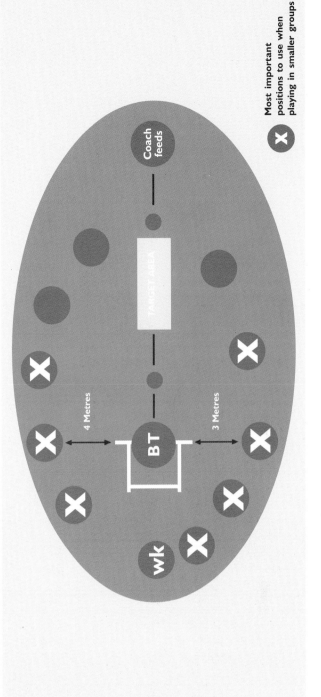

PLAYERS MUST ONLY PLAY DEFENSIVE SHOTS OR THEY ARE OUT (SAFETY)

AIM OF THE GAME

To see which team or individual survives the most deliveries. This simulates playing out for a draw and saving a game.

THE PULL SHOT

This is an attacking shot played to a short-pitched ball that bounces between the batsman's waist and chest height.
The line of the ball is on off to outside leg stump. This shot is played to spin bowlers or a medium pacer — NOT A FAST BOWLER.
(Ideal shot to use against a leg spin bowler who drops one short.)

Initial sideways position

Open front leg position, becoming chest on to the bowler

Transfer weight from back leg to splayed front leg

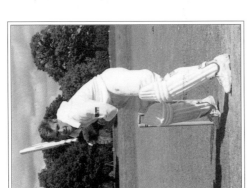

Head still throughout the shot, bat swings over leading shoulder

HANDS SWING HORIZONTALLY THROUGH 360° (A FULL CIRCLE)
KEEP THE HEAD STILL THROUGHOUT THE SHOT

Rear shoulder now points up the wicket

Bat swings horizontally to hit the ball at arm's length

Feet in line, body chest on to bowler

Deep step back into crease

FROM A HIGH BACKLIFT, HIT DOWNWARDS USING THE FULL FACE OF THE BAT
DON'T TRY TO ROLL THE WRISTS — THIS WILL HAPPEN NATURALLY

STEP-BY-STEP ACCOUNT OF HOW TO PLAY THE PULL SHOT

BACKLIFT, AND STEPPING BACK INTO LINE

As the bowler is about to deliver the ball:

1. With a dominant top hand and relaxed bottom hand, pick up bat over off stump, open bat face slightly.
- Push hands up behind back hip pocket
- Create diamond shape with arms
- Leading elbow bent at 90°, pointing down wicket
- Free rear arm from body
- Bottom hand fingers and thumb grip

2. From initial sideways position, dip head and shoulder towards the ball. Push off front leg, open leading shoulder, step back and across the crease. GET HEAD ON OR INSIDE THE LINE OF THE BALL!
- Leave hands high up behind back hip pocket
- Back foot points to mid off
- Weight should be on back foot
- Head forward of body
- Now you *have* decided *to play the pull shot*

3. Transfer weight from back foot to front foot. Hips and chest now pointing up wicket, feet spread and in line with each other.
- Leave hands high up behind back hip pocket
- Weight transferred to front foot
- Head forward of body

EXECUTING THE PULL SHOT

THINK: FROM A HIGH BACKLIFT, HIT THE BALL DOWNWARDS

4. From top of backlift, tuck rear arm into your body and SWING bat horizontally across body to hit the ball. Hold bat firmly in palm of bottom hand.
- Bottom hand dominant, top hand guides
- Head forward of body pointing down wicket
- Bat horizontal to ground

5. Strike the ball at arm's length with bat horizontal directly in front of stomach. Use full face of bat and keep weight on splayed front foot as shot is played.
- Keep head pointing down wicket
- Hips and chest facing bowler
- Hit downwards from high backlift
- Arms straight on impact with ball

6. Complete follow-through with arms swinging over leading shoulder and chest now facing square leg. DO NOT TRY TO ROLL THE WRISTS — THIS OCCURS NATURALLY.
- Keep head in same position
- Move body weight towards square leg area
- Bat finishes parallel to ground

AIM — TO HIT THE BALL BETWEEN MID WICKET AND SQUARE LEG, ALONG THE GROUND

GROUP COACHING FOR THE PULL SHOT

THINK! ENJOYMENT MINIMISES BOREDOM AND ENCOURAGES REPETITION (REPETITION → DEVELOPMENT)

IMPORTANT OVERALL TIPS FOR THE COACH

SAFETY (MOST IMPORTANT)

1. Use Wind Balls®, Incrediballs® or tennis balls. NEVER USE CRICKET BALLS INDOORS WHEN GROUP COACHING. Cricket balls should be used outdoors only, and only with competent players.

2. (a) Always make sure there is a good distance between each group.
   (b) Always make sure each group hits the ball away from each other or into walls.
   (c) Always look for potential dangers. Keep an eye on your suspect players, and position yourself where you can see everybody.
   (d) Don't let fielders stand too close to the batsmen.
   (e) Be strict on safety and punish offenders (i.e. sit-ups, press-ups, etc.); but always have fun.
   (f) Maintain an authoritative voice so that you are always heard.

MOTIVATION

3. (a) Give plenty of praise before constructive criticism.
   (b) Be strict but humorous and always have fun.
   (c) Conclude practice with praise about positive improvement.

COACHING PROGRESSION

4. Always follow practice with a conditioned competitive game of what you have been working on.

SUMMARY OF PRACTICE

5. Recap of coaching points, plus encouragement and praise.

DEMONSTRATION OF SHOT AND PRACTICE WITH GROUP

5 minutes maximum and don't waffle
Project your voice, and be precise and to the point
Coach should always have his bat with him!

The coach explains the pull shot with players sat in front of him. It is an ATTACKING SHOT played off the back foot to a long hop bowled by a spinner. It is a positive shot used to put away a bad ball. This shot can be played at any time in your innings. It is played to a ball which is short-pitched and bounces between knee and waist height (long hop). The line of the ball would be from middle to outside leg stump. NEVER PLAY THIS SHOT TO FAST BOWLERS!

1. Coach executes silent demonstration without the ball, once side on, once front on.

2. Coach executes slow-motion demonstration, once side on, once front on, and introduces one or two coaching points.

3. Coach numbers off groups and sets up first group to show how practice works; others watch. (Put left-handers in the same group, if possible.)

4. Coach takes place of batsman in demonstration group and executes the shot, with the ball, one last time (explaining line, length and bounce of feed).

5. When first group is operational coach goes round and sets up other groups. MONITOR ALL GROUPS AT ALL TIMES — SAFETY.

SET UP FOR THE PRACTICE

1. Set up practice as shown below.
2. Target area: 10–15 metres away from batsman — SAFETY.
3. Target area: 10–15 metres wide. NOTE — FOR BETTER PLAYERS TARGET AREA SHOULD BE FURTHER AWAY.
4. Mark out target area on the floor for feeder to aim at.
5. Ideal number for groups is 6–8 players — MAXIMUM ACTIVITY.
6. Feeder stands 10–12 paces from batsman.
7. Feeder says "Bat up!", then feeds a DART FEED, which bounces once between the batsman's waist and chest height on leg stump line. (From head height throw downwards.)
8. Each group has 3 balls.
9. Ideal duration of practice: 20–30 minutes.

RULES OF THE PRACTICE

1. Each player has 8–10 feeds, then all rotate clockwise.
2. Give groups 2–3 coaching points to work on.
3. Have about 3–4 rounds each (depending on time limit).
4. All rounds of 8–10 to be played with two hands, but stress the importance of the dominant bottom hand.
5. Make the last round of 8–10 competitive: try to hit all balls through the target area along the ground. Fielders must stop the ball.
6. If players leave the ball they get another feed. If they play and miss they don't.
7. If players hit the ball into the air, over the fielders, it doesn't count and they lose that feed.
8. On the competitive round, if a player gets out all change round.

ALWAYS PLAY THE PULL SHOT INTO A WALL, AND DON'T SET UP GROUPS TOO CLOSE TO ONE ANOTHER — THINK SAFETY!
COACH POSITIONS HIMSELF WHERE HE CAN MONITOR ALL GROUPS SAFELY

COACHING POINTS (IN ORDER OF IMPORTANCE)

For younger players, introduce one point at a time.

1. High backlift over off stump with dominant top hand. (Bottom hand fingers and thumb grip.)
2. Step back and across the crease, getting head and body into line with the ball (eyes level).
3. Weight initially on back foot, with head forward of body. Front foot opens out towards leg side, landing in line with back foot. (Batsman now chest on to bowler.)
4. Prior to striking the ball, weight transfers to splayed front leg.
5. Strike the ball at arm's length, head slightly forward of body.
6. From a high backlift, hit downwards with dominant bottom hand.
7. Aim to hit the ball downwards, just in front of square leg.
8. Weight finishes towards square leg, head still pointing up the wicket.

REMEMBER: TIME THE BALL WITH CORRECT TECHNIQUE — DON'T TRY TO HIT IT TOO HARD

OUTSIDE

Fielders positioned in target area, as shown (20-25 metres away)

INDOORS, IN SMALL SPORTS HALLS

Fielders can stand to the batsman's off side, to field rebounds off the wall
Batsman stands closer to the wall (10 metres)

INDOORS

Always use corners of sports hall to set up groups for the pull shot
No more than four groups — SAFETY

20 Metres
10 metres
TARGET AREA
10 metres Rebound Method
Ball must bounce once from dart feed
Rebound fielders

FLD FLD FLD
Feeder
wk
BT
FLD FLD FLD

AIM OF THE PRACTICE

To pull the ball successfully towards the target area. This shows you how to hit the long hop off the back foot against spin bowling. This practice can be turned into a conditioned game for teams/individuals by adding running between wickets, playing the same rules as for front/back foot driving games.

GARY PALMER CRICKET ACADEMY

STEP-BY-STEP ACCOUNT OF HOW TO PLAY THE CUT SHOT

BACKLIFT, AND STEPPING BACK AND ACROSS

As the bowler is about to deliver the ball:

1. With a dominant top hand and relaxed bottom hand, pick up bat over off stump, open bat face slightly.

- Push hands up behind back hip pocket
- Create diamond shape with arms
- Leading elbow bent at 90°, pointing down wicket
- Free rear arm from body
- Bottom hand finger and thumb grip

2. From sideways position, dip head and shoulder towards the ball. Push off front leg, step back and further across crease than normal towards the line of the ball. You will never get your eyes directly behind the line of the ball, because it is too wide of the off stump.

- Eyes level
- Head and body lean towards cover point
- Leave hands high up behind back hip pocket
- *Now you have decided to play the cut shot*

3. Plant back foot parallel to the crease, bend back leg slightly and turn your leading shoulder towards cover point. Tuck your bottom hand into body, holding handle of bat firmly in palm of hand.

- Weight on slightly bent back leg
- Bottom hand dominant, top hand guides

EXECUTING THE CUT SHOT

THINK! FROM A HIGH BACKLIFT, HIT THE BALL DOWNWARDS

4. From top of backlift, tuck your bottom arm into your body. Pull the bat back horizontally behind your rear shoulder and SWING the bat towards the ball.

- Bottom hand dominant, top hand guides
- Head above back foot
- Forearms horizontal

5. Strike the ball level with your rear shoulder, with the full face of the bat. Keep weight on back foot, but directed towards cover point.

- Dominant bottom hand
- Wrists roll automatically

6. Complete follow-through with arms swinging over leading shoulder and chest still pointing at cover point.

- Keep head in same position
- Body weight finishes towards cover point
- Bat finishes parallel to ground

DON'T CUT STRAIGHT, SHORT-PITCHED DELIVERIES THAT ARE CLOSE TO YOUR BODY

ONLY CUT BALLS WIDE OF OFF STUMP

Aim - to hit the ball just infront of cover point

THE CUT SHOT

This shot is an attacking shot played to a short-pitched ball which is wide outside off stump and bounces between waist and chest height. It is generally used against medium pace and fast bowlers, to put away a bad ball.

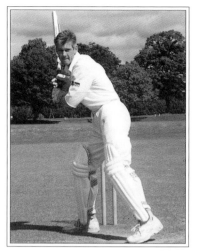

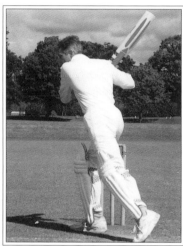
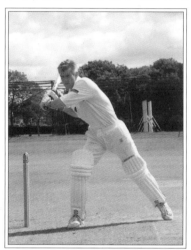
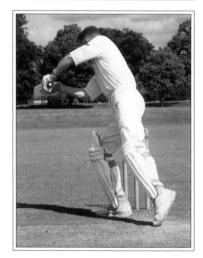

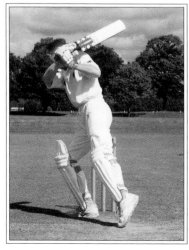

THE HOOK SHOT

This is an attacking shot, generally used against a fast bowler when he bowls you a "bouncer". A bouncer is a very short-pitched delivery that bounces between the batsman's chest and head height. This shot is best played when the line of the ball is around leg stump or just outside.

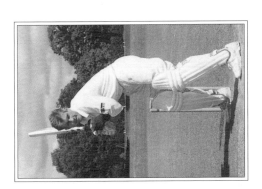

IF THE BALL RISES MORE THAN EXPECTED, GET UP ONTO YOUR TOES (RISE WITH THE BALL) TO PLAY THE SHOT

HANDS AND ARMS SWING HORIZONTALLY THROUGH 360° (A FULL CIRCLE)

HIPS TURN THROUGH 180° TO FACE THE OPPOSITE DIRECTION

KEEP THE HEAD STILL THROUGHOUT THE SHOT

AIM — TO HIT THE BALL BETWEEN SQUARE LEG AND MIDWICKET

NOTE — The hook is played most successfully when you have been at the crease for some time and have played yourself in. To hit a six just get inside and underneath the ball more, and hit upwards more.

STEP-BY-STEP ACCOUNT OF HOW TO PLAY THE HOOK SHOT

BACKLIFT, AND STEPPING BACK INTO LINE

As the bowler is about to deliver the ball:

1. **With a dominant top hand and relaxed bottom hand, pick up bat over off stump, open bat face slightly.**
   - Lift hands up behind back hip pocket
   - Create diamond shape with arms
   - Leading elbow bent at 90°, pointing down wicket
   - Free rear arm from body
   - Bottom hand fingers and thumb grip

2. **From initial sideways position, dip head and shoulder towards the ball. Push off front leg and step back and across the crease, with body weight directed towards the cover point. GET HEAD AND BODY INSIDE THE LINE OF THE BALL!**
   - Backlift remains raised high above off stump
   - Head still, eyes level

3. **As leading shoulder begins to open, rear arm tucks into body and bottom hand takes control. Weight now on back foot.**
   - Back foot points towards mid off
   - Get up onto toes
   - Head still, eyes level

EXECUTING THE HOOK SHOT

THINK! FROM A HIGH BACKLIFT, HIT THE BALL DOWNWARDS

4. **From top of backlift, SWING bat horizontally across body towards the ball. Pivot on back foot as front leg naturally swings in an arc past back leg.**
   - Body naturally pivots on back leg
   - Chest and hips start opening towards ball
   - Toes of front foot resting lightly on the ground
   - Forearms horizontal to ground

5. **Strike the ball at arm's length with a dominant BOTTOM HAND and the FULL face of the bat. KEEP HEAD AND BODY INSIDE THE LINE OF THE BALL!**
   - Keep head still, eyes level
   - Rise up onto your toes
   - Hit downwards from high backlift

6. **Complete follow-through with hips and chest pointing towards fine leg area. Bat finishes over leading shoulder.**
   - Leading shoulder finishes behind body
   - Bat finishes parallel to ground (swings through 360°)
   - Body pivots naturally on back foot
   - Head still throughout the shot, eyes level

NEVER TAKE YOUR EYES OFF THE BALL WHEN HOOKING IT!

THE SWEEP SHOT

This is an attacking shot played to a good length ball on or outside leg stump. It is mainly played against spin bowlers. It is safer to play this shot against an off spinner than any other spinner, as there is less chance of getting out LBW.

Head still throughout shot

Front pad in line with ball

Bottom hand controls shot

STEP-BY-STEP ACCOUNT OF HOW TO PLAY THE SWEEP SHOT

BACKLIFT AND STEPPING FORWARD INTO LINE

As the bowler is about to deliver the ball:

1. With a dominant top hand and relaxed bottom hand, pick up bat over or off stump, open bat face slightly.
- Push hands up behind back hip pocket
- Create diamond shape with arms
- Leading elbow bent at 90°, pointing down wicket
- Free rear arm from body
- Bottom hand fingers and thumb grip

2. From initial sideways position, lean towards the ball with head and shoulders forward of body and back foot still raised above off stump.
- Eyes level
- Leave hands high up behind back hip pocket

3. Take a long stride down the line of leg stump and get as close to the pitch of the ball as possible. Put your front pad IN LINE with the ball. Bend front knee so your back knee touches the ground.
- Head in line with ball, eyes level
- Head above front knee
- Weight on front foot

EXECUTING THE SWEEP SHOT

THINK! DON'T TRY TO HIT THE BALL TOO HARD

4. From top of backlift, push your hands and bat towards cover point, and SWING bat out ahead of front knee, horizontally across your front knee.
- Swing bat ahead of body
- Keep arms relaxed
- Bottom hand controls shot, top hand guides

5. Swing bat out ahead of you close to the ground and make contact with the ball at arm's length and directly in line with the front pad. Hit downwards.
- Head still, eyes level
- Arms fully stretched
- Bottom hand dominant, top hand guides

6. Complete follow-through with forearms across front pad and rear shoulder pointing down wicket.
- Head points down the wicket
- Arms fully stretched throughout
- Chest finishes pointing at mid wicket

GET INTO A LOW POSITION WITH A LONG STRIDE TO THE BALL, WITH YOUR FRONT FOOT FORWARD OF YOUR HEAD POSITION

Chest points to leg side on completion of shot

Back leg touching the ground

Long stride to the ball, front foot further forward than head

DON'T TRY TO HIT THE BALL — JUST HELP IT ON ITS WAY BEHIND SQUARE

WHEN SWEEPING THE BALL TURNING AWAY FROM THE BAT, GET YOUR PAD INSIDE THE LINE OF THE BALL

GROUP COACHING FOR THE CUT, HOOK AND SWEEP

SUGGESTED WAYS TO PRACTISE THE CUT, HOOK AND SWEEP SHOTS SAFELY IN A GROUP (USE WIND BALLS®, INCREDIBALLS® OR TENNIS BALLS)

The leg glances are continuations of the back and front foot defence and both are difficult to feed. The flick off the legs front and back foot are continuations of the back and front foot on drive and are also difficult to feed. The above shots are more advanced shots that you will naturally master in your own time. Look at the picture cards to show you the correct technique. Master the basic defence and drives, and the flicks and glances will look after themselves.

CUT

FEED A ONE-BOUNCE DART FEED FROM (A) KNEELING OR (B) STANDING UP

THROW THE FEED WITH PACE OUTSIDE OFF STUMP BETWEEN WAIST AND CHEST HEIGHT

Rebound fielders

TARGET AREA

Inside: at least metres
Outside or in a large hall: at least 15 metres

LINE OF FEED

FEEDER

WK

IN A SMALL SPORTS HALL

HIT INTO A WALL AND FIELDERS WILL GET THE REBOUND.
IMPORTANT — NO FIELDERS WITHIN THE TARGET AREA. BATSMAN STANDS AT LEAST 5 METRES FROM THE WALL.

OUTSIDE OR IN A LARGE SPORTS HALL

FIELDERS STAND WITHIN THE TARGET AREA, AT LEAST 15 METRES FROM THE BATSMAN.

HOOK

FOR THIS SHOT WEAR A HELMET, FOR SAFETY AND REALISM

(A) FEED A ONE-BOUNCE DART FEED FROM STANDING UP (THROW THE FEED WITH PACE SO IT BOUNCES BETWEEN CHEST AND HEAD HEIGHT); OR (B) FIELD FROM ONE KNEE, UNDERARM THROW UPWARDS, AROUND SHOULDER HEIGHT (NO BOUNCE)

Rebound fielders

FEEDER

LINE OF FEED

WK

TARGET AREA

Inside: at least 8 metres
Outside or in a large hall: at least 15 metres

IN A SMALL SPORTS HALL

HIT INTO A WALL AND FIELDERS WILL GET THE REBOUND OR CATCH.
IMPORTANT — NO FIELDERS WITHIN THE TARGET AREA. BATSMAN STANDS AT LEAST 8 METRES FROM THE WALL.

OUTSIDE OR IN A LARGE SPORTS HALL

FIELDERS STAND WITHIN THE TARGET AREA, AT LEAST 15 METRES FROM THE BATSMAN.

SWEEP

FEED A ONE-BOUNCE UNDERARM FROM (A) STANDING UP OR (B) BOBBLE FEED

THROW A LENGTH BALL SLOWLY ON LEG STUMP WHICH BOUNCES AROUND KNEE HEIGHT

Rebound fielders

FEEDER

LINE OF FEED

WK

Inside: at least 5 metres
Outside or in a large hall: at least 10 metres

TARGET AREA

IN A SMALL SPORTS HALL

HIT INTO A WALL AND FIELDERS WILL GET THE REBOUND.
IMPORTANT — NO FIELDERS WITHIN THE TARGET AREA. BATSMAN STANDS AT LEAST 5 METRES FROM THE WALL.

OUTSIDE OR IN A LARGE SPORTS HALL

FIELDERS STAND WITHIN THE TARGET AREA, AT LEAST 10 METRES FROM THE BATSMAN.

GARY PALMER CRICKET ACADEMY

THE LEG GLANCE OFF THE FRONT FOOT

This is a scoring shot played to a good length ball pitching on or just inside the line of leg stump and bouncing between knee and waist height. You must use the pace of the ball for this shot, and steer it down towards the fine leg area. A useful, low-risk shot against fast bowlers.

Front foot inside the line of the ball

Bat face begins to close towards the leg side

Toe of bat points up the wicket on completion of the shot (high hands and leading elbow)

Let the ball come out make contact with the ball forward of your front foot

Dip head and shoulder and take a short stride to the ball

Strike ball with top spin motion — created by the WRISTS

DO NOT HIT ACROSS THE LINE OF THE BALL — KEEP THE BAT STRAIGHT!

STEP-BY-STEP ACCOUNT OF HOW TO PLAY THE FRONT FOOT LEG GLANCE

1. With a dominant top hand and relaxed bottom hand, pick up bat over off stump, open bat face slightly.
- Push hands up behind back hip pocket
- Create diamond shape with arms
- Leading elbow bent at 90°, pointing down the wicket
- Free rear arm from body
- Bottom hand holds bat with fingers and thumb only

2. Open leading shoulder as for the on drive. Maintain more open body position and dip head and shoulder towards the ball.
- Eyes level
- Head forward of body
- Leave hands up behind back hip pocket

3. Take a SHORT STRIDE and plant your front foot INSIDE the line of the ball. Toe of front foot points up the wicket.
- Bend front knee, back leg straight
- Stand tall
- Head forward of body (eyes level)
- Weight on ball of front foot
- Maintain raised backlift

EXECUTING THE FRONT FOOT LEG GLANCE

THINK! LET THE BALL COME AND STEER IT DOWN TOWARDS FINE LEG WITH CORRECT TECHNIQUE

4. From top of backlift, PUSH arms and bat face in a direct line towards the ball. Arms pass close to the body and bat face begins to close towards the leg side.
- Arms maintain diamond shape throughout
- Keep arms relaxed
- Keep hands high
- Top hand dominates initially
- Bottom hand relaxed fingers and thumb grip

5. With elbow close to head and high hands, make contact with the ball just before it passes the outside of the front thigh. Turn hands and bat face towards NEARSIDE HALF of the ball. Bottom hand with fingers and thumb grip steers the ball towards fine leg.
- Bottom hand pushes bat face towards square leg
- Head inside the line of the ball (eyes level)
- Hands forward of bat face on impact
- Diamond shape still maintained with arms
- Bottom hand finishes above top hand on completion of shot

AIM — TO LET THE BALL BRUSH ACROSS THE BAT FACE SO YOU CAN STEER IT TOWARDS THE FINE LEG AREA

THE FRONT FOOT FLICK OFF THE LEGS

This is a scoring shot played to a half volley, pitching on or just outside the line of leg stump and bouncing around and below knee height. It is an attacking shot where you use the pace of the ball as well as striking it with a top spin motion created by the bottom hand. Aim to hit half the ball with a glancing blow across the face of the bat. A useful low-risk shot against fast bowlers.

Toe of bat points directly upwards on completion of the shot (high hands and leading elbow)

Bat face begins to close towards the leg side

Front foot inside the line of the ball

Dip head and shoulder and take a short stride to the ball

Let the ball come but make contact with it forward of your front foot

Strike ball with top spin motion — created by the ARMS

DO NOT HIT ACROSS THE LINE OF THE BALL — KEEP THE BAT STRAIGHT!

STEP-BY-STEP ACCOUNT OF HOW TO PLAY THE FRONT FOOT FLICK OFF THE LEGS

1. With a dominant top hand and relaxed bottom hand, pick up bat over off stump, open bat face slightly.
   - Push hands up behind back hip pocket
   - Create diamond shape with arms
   - Leading elbow bent at 90°, pointing down the wicket
   - Free rear arm from body
   - Bottom hand holds bat with fingers and thumb only

2. Open leading shoulder as for the on drive. Maintain more open body position and dip head and shoulders towards the ball.
   - Eyes level
   - Head forward of body
   - Leave hands up behind back hip pocket

3. Take a SHORT STRIDE and plant your front foot INSIDE the line of the ball. Toe of front foot points up the wicket on the line of leg stump.
   - Bend front knee, back leg straight
   - Stand tall
   - Head forward of body (eyes level)
   - Weight on ball of front foot
   - Maintain raised backlift

EXECUTING THE FRONT FOOT FLICK OFF THE LEGS

DON'T TRY TO HIT THE BALL TOO HARD

THINK! LET THE BALL COME AND STROKE IT WITH CORRECT TECHNIQUE

4. From top of backlift, SWING arms and bat face in a direct line towards the ball. Swing bat down the line of mid wicket. Bat face begins to close towards square leg area as it swings towards the ball.
   - Arms maintain diamond shape throughout
   - Keep arms relaxed
   - Top hand controls swing of bat to ball
   - Bottom hand relaxed fingers and thumb grip

5. Strike NEARSIDE HALF of the ball with TOP SPIN motion created by the bottom hand, just before it passes the outside of the front pad.
   - Bottom hand pushes upwards on impact (top spin motion)
   - Head directly over ball (eyes level)
   - Hands forward of bat face on impact
   - Bat face points towards leg side

6. Complete follow-through with hands high ABOVE leading elbow. Toe of bat points directly upwards.
   - Diamond shape still maintained with arms
   - Bottom hand fingers and thumb grip
   - Bottom hand finishes above top hand on completion of shot

AIM — TO HIT THE BALL BETWEEN MID WICKET AND SQUARE LEG

THE LEG GLANCE OFF THE BACK FOOT

This is a scoring shot played to a short-pitched ball on or just outside the line of leg stump and bouncing between waist and chest height. You must use the pace of the ball for this shot. A useful low-risk shot against fast bowlers on bouncy wickets.

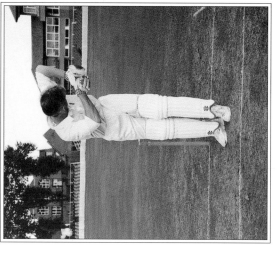

Get body inside the line of the ball

Toe of bat points up the wicket on completion of the shot (high hands and leading elbow)

Front leg opens out slightly and bat face begins to close towards the leg side

Let the ball come and make contact forward of your body (high elbow)

Dip head and shoulder towards the ball

Strike ball with top spin motion — created by the WRISTS

DO NOT HIT ACROSS THE LINE OF THE BALL — KEEP THE BAT STRAIGHT!

STEP-BY-STEP ACCOUNT OF HOW TO PLAY THE BACK FOOT LEG GLANCE

1. With a dominant top hand and relaxed bottom hand, pick up bat over off stump, open bat face slightly.
- Push hands up behind back hip pocket
- Create diamond shape with arms
- Leading elbow bent at 90°, pointing down the wicket
- Free rear arm from body
- Bottom hand holds bat with fingers and thumb only

2. From sideways position, dip head and shoulder towards the ball. Push off front leg, and step back and across the crease, maintaining backlift. GET INSIDE THE LINE OF THE BALL.
- Maintain raised backlift
- Eyes level
- Head still, forward of body
- Head and shoulder pointing down the wicket

3. Plant back foot pointing towards cover, open leading shoulder slightly and maintain more open body position throughout the shot. (Front leg slides towards back leg, acting as a counterbalance.)
- Weight initially on back foot, head over front foot
- Stand tall
- Head forward of body (eyes level)
- Leading shoulder opens, points towards MID ON
- Back leg covers middle and off stump

EXECUTING THE BACK FOOT LEG GLANCE

THINK! LET THE BALL COME AND STEER IT DOWN TOWARDS FINE LEG WITH CORRECT TECHNIQUE

4. From top of backlift, PUSH arms and bat face in a direct line towards the body. Arms pass close to the body and bat face begins to close towards the leg side.
- Arms maintain diamond shape throughout
- Keep arms relaxed
- Top hand dominates initially
- Bottom hand relaxed, fingers and thumb grip

5. With elbow close to head and high hands, make contact with the ball just before it passes your ribs. Turn hands and bat face towards NEARSIDE HALF of the ball. Bottom hand with fingers and thumb grip steers the ball towards fine leg.
- Bottom hand pushes bat face towards square leg
- Head inside the line of the ball (eyes level)
- Hands forward of bat face on impact
- Diamond shape still maintained with arms
- Bottom hand finishes above top hand on completion of shot

AIM — TO LET THE BALL BRUSH ACROSS THE BAT FACE SO YOU CAN STEER IT TOWARDS THE FINE LEG AREA

THE BACK FOOT FLICK OFF THE LEGS

This is a scoring shot played to a short-pitched ball on or just outside the line of leg stump and bouncing between knee and waist height.
It is an attacking shot where you use the pace of the ball as well as striking it with a top spin motion created by the bottom hand.
Aim to hit half the ball with a glancing blow across the face of the bat. A useful low-risk shot against fast bowlers.

Get body inside the line of the ball

Bat face begins to close towards the leg side

Dip head and shoulder towards the ball

Body inside line of ball; transfer weight to front foot, let the ball come, strike ball forward of body

Toe of bat points directly upwards on completion of the shot (high hands and leading elbow)

Strike ball with top spin motion — created by the ARMS (high hands)

DO NOT HIT ACROSS THE LINE OF THE BALL — KEEP THE BAT STRAIGHT!

STEP-BY-STEP ACCOUNT OF HOW TO PLAY THE BACK FOOT FLICK OFF THE LEGS

1. With a dominant top hand and relaxed bottom hand, pick up bat over off stump, open bat face slightly.
- Push hands up behind back hip pocket
- Create diamond shape with arms
- Leading elbow bent at 90°, pointing down the wicket
- Free rear arm from body
- Bottom hand holds bat with fingers and thumb only

2. From sideways position, dip head and shoulder towards the ball. Push off front leg and step back and across the crease. GET INSIDE THE LINE OF THE BALL.
- Maintain raised backlift
- Eyes level
- Head still, forward of body
- Head and shoulder pointing down the wicket

3. Plant back foot pointing towards cover, open leading shoulder slightly and maintain more open body position throughout the shot. (Front leg slides towards back leg, acting as a counterbalance.)
- Weight initially on back foot, head over front foot
- Stand tall
- Head forward of body (eyes level)
- Leading shoulder opens, points towards MID ON
- Back leg covers middle and off stump

EXECUTING THE BACK FOOT FLICK OFF THE LEGS

DON'T TRY TO HIT THE BALL TOO HARD

THINK! LET THE BALL COME AND STROKE IT WITH CORRECT TECHNIQUE

4. From top of backlift, SWING arms and bat face towards mid wicket with arms passing close to body. Transfer weight onto front foot ready to strike.
- Arms maintain diamond shape throughout swing
- Keep arms relaxed
- Top hand controls initial swing of bat
- Bottom hand relaxed, fingers and thumb grip

5. Strike NEARSIDE HALF of the ball with a TOP SPIN motion created by the bottom hand, just before it passes the outside of the front pad.
- Bottom hand pushes upwards on impact (top spin motion)
- Head directly over ball (eyes level)
- Hands forward of bat face on impact
- Bat face points towards square leg

6. Complete follow-through with hands high ABOVE leading elbow. Toe of bat points directly upwards.
- Diamond shape still maintained with arms
- Bottom hand fingers and thumb grip
- Bottom hand finishes above top hand on completion of shot

AIM — TO HIT THE BALL BETWEEN MID WICKET AND SQUARE LEG

GARY PALMER CRICKET ACADEMY

PLAYING THE BOUNCER

This is a ball which is very short (i.e. half-way down the wicket), and bounces above shoulder height. Generally, against fast bowlers, you duck and sway. If the ball is short and bouncing over middle and leg stump, try to duck. If the ball is short and bouncing over off stump, you should sway.

SWAYING

GET BACK AND ACROSS IN LINE WITH THE BALL, THEN SWAY (OFF STUMP LINE DELIVERIES)

1. Step back in the crease, getting your head and body in line with the ball.

2. Leave your head forward of the body.

3. Weight on the back foot with head over the front foot.

4. Let your front foot slide to meet your back foot.

5. Stand tall in a sideways position and WATCH THE BALL.

6. With head forward of leading shoulder, lean away and let the ball go past you.

7. Drop your hands down close to your body so they are out of the way of the ball.

8. If the ball bounces higher than you expect, get up onto your toes.

KEEP WATCHING THE BALL — NEVER TAKE YOUR EYES OFF IT!

DUCKING

GET BACK AND ACROSS INSIDE THE LINE OF THE BALL, THEN DUCK (LEG STUMP LINE DELIVERIES)

1. Step back in the crease, getting your head and body in line with the ball.

2. Leave your head forward of the body.

3. Weight on the back foot with head over the front foot.

4. Let your front foot slide to meet your back foot. If you pick up the bouncer early enough (i.e. you step back as you are ducking), then your feet will be spread.

5. QUICKLY, bend both knees and duck underneath the ball.

6. Keep your hands low.

KEEP WATCHING THE BALL — NEVER TAKE YOUR EYES OFF IT!

Take a good step back in the crease — Back foot must stay parallel, you must stay sideways

Head must be still — Don't take your eye off the ball!

HAVE CONFIDENCE IN YOUR NATURAL REACTIONS! Don't look for the bouncer or prejudge it — You will get out of the way naturally, by instinct

THINK! "THE QUICKER THEY BOWL, THE BRAVER I WILL BE"

36

(A) FRONT FOOT SHOTS ONLY   (B) BACK FOOT SHOTS ONLY   (C) MIXED AT RANDOM   (in order of difficulty)

NEVER PLAY AN ATTACKING SHOT THROUGH SQUARE LEG WHEN PRACTISING THIS EXERCISE

FEEDING PROGRESSION

Try to feed the ball on off stump line or just outside.

(a) Bobble Feed — Front foot drives

(b) Underarm, One Bounce — Front foot drive and defence

(c) Dart Feed (throw from near ear downwards, one bounce) —
 (i) Back foot defence and drive
 (ii) Front or back foot

(d) Underarm Leg Spin — Front or back foot

(e) Dart Feed Off Break (give the ball air) — Front or back foot

Use any of these feeding progressions, starting with the easier ones.

LAYOUT

1. Set up groups as shown opposite: one batsman, one wicket keeper, one feeder and one or two fielders.

2. Mark out the V area with chalk or discs, approximately 4–5 metres wide.

3. For more talented players move the marker on the off side further in, to make the V more narrow.

4. Ideally, practise this in the nets, in groups of three: batsman, feeder, wicket keeper. (Hit the ball towards the back of the net, from the bowler's end.)

RULES OF THE GAME

You must play a straight-batted shot, otherwise you are out.

If you hit the ball in the V or leave it, it counts as a run. If you hit it outside the markers, you are out.

The feeder must think like a bowler and try to get the batter to play a widish delivery around the offstump line thus hitting the ball outside the target area on the offside.

PRACTICE

1. First, give each batsman a set number of deliveries (e.g. 15 or 25).

2. If the batsman is out, score –2.

PROGRESSION

3. Progress to batting until all players are out, then change round.

4. Make the V more narrow for more competent players.

5. Set a number of runs at which a batsman must retire.

WAYS OF GETTING OUT

1. Caught

2. Bowled

3. Stumped

4. Hitting the ball outside the V

5. Hitting the ball into the air

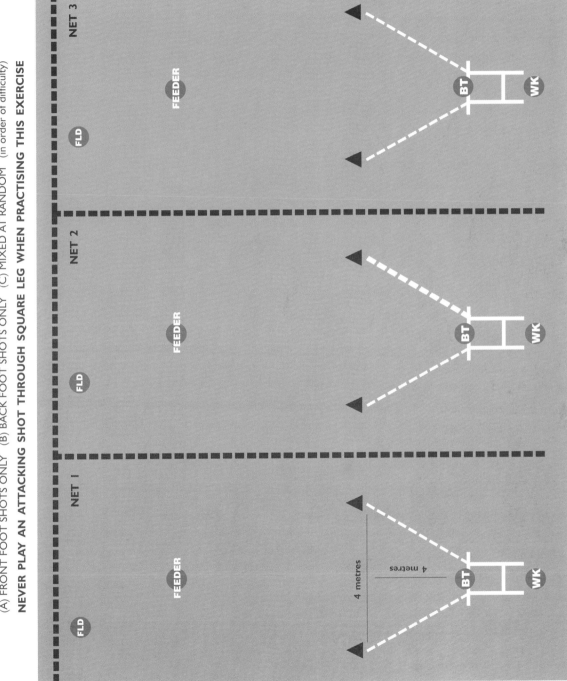

NET 1 | NET 2 | NET 3

4 metres

4 metres

AIMS

The feeder has to lure the batsman to strike the ball outside of the markers. He must get the batsman to play at the straight deliveries and then gradually start feeding the ball wider until the batsman plays at a wide delivery and hits the ball to the outside of the marked area.

BATSMEN — To teach the batsman to leave the ball wide of off stump; also to teach him to drive the ball along the ground, straighter rather than wider.

FEEDERS — To teach them to think like bowlers, trying to make the batsman play at a wide delivery and get caught behind.

DON'T TRY TO HIT THE BALL TOO HARD — TIME IT!

RUNNING BETWEEN THE WICKETS

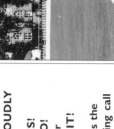

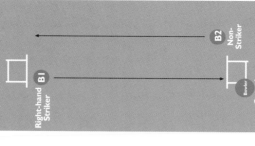

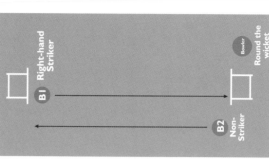

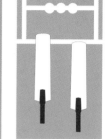

**CALL EARLY
AND LOUDLY**

**YES!
NO!
or
WAIT!**

**NO! is the
overriding call**

STRIKER: Never run straight up the wicket —
Always run to your OFF SIDE

Right-hand
Striker
B1

B2
Non-
Striker

Over the
wicket

Bowler

Right-hand
Striker
B1

Round the
wicket

Bowler

B2
Non-
Striker

AREA A

Striker

AREA B

Non-striker

AREA A: Non-striker calls
AREA B: Striker calls

Bat must be grounded
over popping crease

Don't move out of the crease until the bowler has released the ball, then back up approximately 1 metre

Always face the ball when turning, change hands, hold end of bat handle and get low to reach for the crease

Always run the bat in along the ground about one metre from the popping crease

GROUP COACHING FOR RUNNING BETWEEN THE WICKETS

LAYOUT OF PRACTICE

1. Mark out lines on the floor 5 metres apart.
2. All players have a bat.
3. Spread groups out a safe distance apart.
4. Keep them in their lines.

DEMONSTRATION OF RUNNING BETWEEN THE WICKETS

1. Sit group down in front of you.
2. Explain about running between the wickets (8 minutes maximum).
3. Draw lines on the floor with chalk.
4. Demonstrate the various ways of running, depending on what side the ball is hit.
5. Explain that on the line is out.
6. Make them shout the calls back to you. Explain who calls when.
7. Set up first group to demonstrate.
8. Have a few practice runs, then a competitive race.

COACHING POINTS

1. **CALLS: YES! NO! or WAIT!** (NO! is the overriding call.) **CALL LOUDLY AND CLEARLY.**
2. Non-striker calls when the ball goes behind the wicket, as he has the best view. (i.e. through the slips or the fine leg area).
3. Striker calls when the ball is in front of square or through gully area, as he then has the best view.
4. Hold bat at the end of the handle.
5. Change hands — Never turn blind, always face the ball when turning to run another single.
6. Run bat into the crease on every run. On a quick single, run it in a metre before, until it crosses the popping crease.
7. Get low and reach for the crease between runs.
8. Talk to each other when crossing and possibly going to attempt another run (i.e. looking for 2).
9. NEVER GET YOUR FEET OVER THE CREASE when turning for another run. Reach for the line with the bat at arm's length, fully stretched.
10. Non-striker must back up fully at the bowler's end just as he delivers the ball.
11. The striker runs to his off side. The non-striker runs the opposite side.
12. When the bowler bowls round the wicket the non-striker now stands to the side the striker is running but wider.
13. Look to run 2 when the ball goes towards the boundary fielders.
14. Always run the first run fast, to turn 1s into 2s and 2s into 3s!
15. NEVER RUN JUST BECAUSE YOU HAVE HIT A GOOD SHOT!

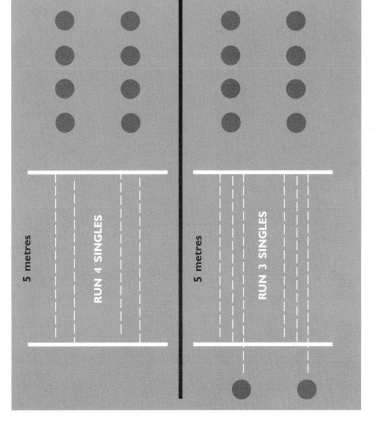

5 metres

RUN 4 SINGLES

5 metres

RUN 3 SINGLES

RULES OF RELAY 1

1. Each batsmen has a bat to carry.
2. All batsmen must run 4 singles facing a particular direction, off or leg side.
3. When the first one has run his bat in the next one can go.
4. If a batsman is short of the line, he must go to the back of the queue and run again.
5. The first team to finish, sit down and shout "Howzat!" wins.

AIMS OF THE PRACTICE

(a) To reach for the line, bat held at the end of the handle.
(b) To change hands and always face the ball — NEVER turning your back on it.
(c) Running the bat in at full arm's length.
(d) Speed between the wickets and quick turning.

RULES OF RELAY 2

1. The first batsman of each group runs a 3.
2. Before they run the coach says what side the ball has been hit.
3. When they have completed 3 runs the coach tells the one who has made the most technical mistakes to go to the back of the queue. The successful runner goes to the other side of the crease. The next runners go on the coach's signal.
4. The first team to get all its players onto the other side wins.

AIMS OF THE PRACTICE

(a) To run the bat in at arm's length.
(b) To change hands and always face the ball — NEVER turning your back on it.
(c) To know how to face the ball, whatever side of the wicket it is hit, and to change hands correctly.
(d) To run between the wickets with good technique.

THE OFF SIDE DRIVING GAME

IDEAL TO PLAY INDOORS, WITH BEGINNERS AND PLAYERS AGED 12 AND UNDER

IF PLAYED OUTSIDE, MARK A BOUNDARY WITH DISCS

LAYOUT FOR THE GAME

NEVER USE CRICKET BALLS INDOORS

USE CRICKET BALLS OUTDOORS ONLY, AND ONLY WITH COMPETENT PLAYERS

1. Set up game as shown opposite. Play as teams of 8–11 a side.

2. The coach feeds:
   - Bobble feeds to very young players
   - Underarm feeds or dart feeds for better/older players

3. Make sure fielders are no closer than 11 yards — SAFETY.

4. Put younger players furthest away from the batsman — SAFETY.

5. Incoming batsmen sit outside the playing area when possible (e.g. in viewing gallery) — SAFETY.

6. Ideal duration of the game: 40–60 minutes.

RULES OF THE GAME

This is like real cricket. The same rules apply, except that:

(a) If you hit the ball on the leg side you are out.

(b) When indoors, you can be caught off the walls, although not off the back wall, which scores 6 runs if hit on the full.

(c) If you hit the ceiling you are out.

(d) No one can field inside the chalk-marked area — SAFETY.

(e) No LBWs.

(f) (i) Two or three balls to score or you are out.
    (ii) Tip and run rules.

(g) Left-handers play on side shots only.

This game can be played with any number of players, from 6 to 16 per side, depending on the size of the hall.

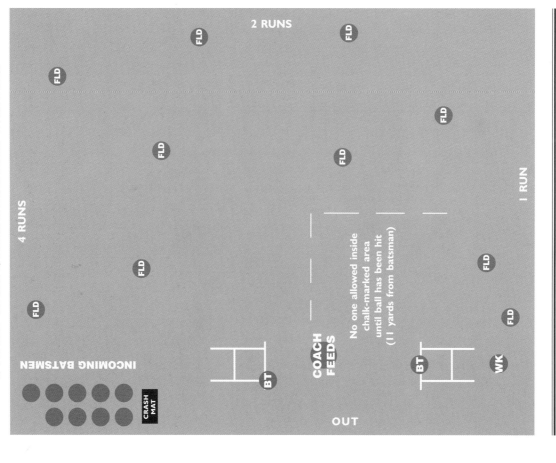

VARIATION OF THE GAME (FOR LARGER SPORTS HALLS)

1. Move the creases so they are in the centre of the hall. NOTE — Fielders must still not be too close on the leg side: 10 metres away — SAFETY.

2. Not out when hitting balls on the leg side (thus incorporating the on drive).

PROGRESSION OF THE GAME

1. Pairs Cricket: 8–10 a side. (See separate coaching sheet on this game.)

2. Play as teams or individual pairs.

3. Every player bowls one over, then rotates. Each pair has 3 or 4 overs (depending on time limit).

4. If you are out you score –6.

5. No batsman faces more than 3 consecutive balls (change them round).

6. Always bowl from the same end.

7. Batsmen change ends at end of over or after the fall of a wicket.

AIMS OF THE PRACTICE

(a) To teach overall aspects of the game of cricket

(b) To simulate a real match type situation

(c) To put into practice the skills you have learned

(d) To strive for good performances

(e) TO ENJOY THE GAME!

THE QUICK SINGLES GAME

EXAMPLE SITUATION FOR THIS WAY OF BATTING

8 OVERS REMAINING, NO WICKETS IN HAND, 30 RUNS TO WIN!

TAKE NO RISKS WITH BIG HITS!

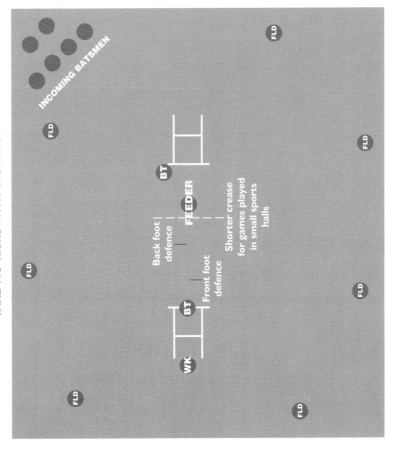

LAYOUT FOR THE GAME

NEVER USE CRICKET BALLS INDOORS

**USE CRICKET BALLS OUTDOORS ONLY,
AND ONLY WITH COMPETENT PLAYERS**

1. Set up game as shown opposite.
2. The coach feeds from approximately 10 paces away.
3. Mark the front foot and back foot target areas on the floor with chalk or markers.
4. Use markers for fielders to stand on or next to.
5. Make sure that the batsman does not bat for too long (e.g. retire at 20) — MAXIMUM ACTIVITY.
6. Position all markers so the batsman can just about run a single without getting out.

NOTE — This game can be played outside using a bowling machine set on a length. But in pairs, each pair has two lives. Excellent practice for County players.

RULES OF THE GAME

1. This game can be played in teams (6–10 a side) or in pairs (8–10 players).
2. Batsmen both ends.
3. If playing in pairs, give each pair two or three lives. If playing in teams, when a wicket falls it is the turn of the next batsman. Tip and run, or two or three balls to make a run.
4. Coach feeds all front foot defence or all back foot defence.
5. Fielders must stay on the cones or with one hand on the wall until the ball is thrown, otherwise batsmen get a 2 run bonus.
6. WAYS OF GETTING OUT: Bowled, caught, run out, stumped, playing an attacking shot, or failing to score off the limited number of deliveries.
7. The batsman can only score singles but the boundaries count for overthrows.
8. Overthrows: side walls = 2 runs, back wall behind wicket keeper = 1 run, front wall = 4 runs. (Unless you hit a 4 you can run singles only to the side and back wall scores).
9. If the batsman leaves the ball it doesn't count and he doesn't have to run.
10. If the batsman plays and misses it counts as a delivery.

PROGRESSION OF THIS GAME

Judging length, front foot or back foot feeds at random.

COACHING POINTS

A. **FOR BATSMEN
(RUNNING BETWEEN THE WICKETS)**

1. Loud, quick positive calling.
2. Changing hands always looking at the ball. Never turning blind.
3. Non-striker backing up.
4. Run the first run fast.
5. Don't run past the crease after one run (because you might have to run again).
6. Run with bat and arm stretched out in front of you.
7. Hold the bat handle at the end.
8. Run your bat in over the line.

B. **FOR FIELDERS
(CREATING PRESSURE, STOPPING SINGLES)**

1. Walking in, THREATENING.
2. Pace to the ball.
3. Watch the ball into your hands under pressure.
4. Always back up other fielders and the wicket keeper.
5. Get to bowler's end to take an incoming throw.
6. Know when not to throw.
7. Know when to throw over the top of the stumps and when to hit them.
8. Remain focused when under pressure.

**THINK! I MUST STOP THE SINGLE AND BUILD PRESSURE FOR THE BATTING SIDE
THEN I WILL FORCE THEM INTO LOSING A WICKET — AND MAYBE THE MATCH?**

AIMS OF THE PRACTICE

A. **FOR BATSMEN**

1. To teach the batsman to judge a quick single and realise how many are available.
2. To show him how to keep a run rate ticking over and how to get off the mark without playing an irrational shot.
3. To show him how to run between the wickets correctly.

B. **FOR FIELDERS**

1. To teach them to execute the underarm flick and attacking interception at speed, under pressure.
2. To show them the importance of backing up.
3. To teach them to create pressure for the batting side and force them into making mistakes (i.e. irrational shots). Fielders can also win matches!

NEVER TEACH YOUNG PLAYERS TO HIT ACROSS THE LINE TO SCORE SINGLES

PAIRS CRICKET

6 A SIDE OR 8 A SIDE

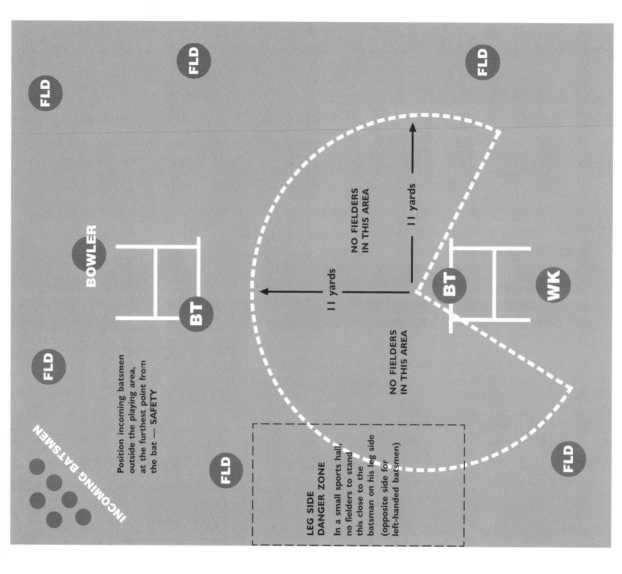

BOWLER

BT

FLD

FLD

FLD

FLD

FLD

FLD

INCOMING BATSMEN

Position incoming batsmen outside the playing area, at the furthest point from the bat — SAFETY

NO FIELDERS IN THIS AREA

11 yards

11 yards

NO FIELDERS IN THIS AREA

BT

WK

LEG SIDE DANGER ZONE

In a small sports hall, no fielders to stand this close to the batsman on his leg side (opposite side for left-handed batsmen)

VARIATION OF THE GAME — 8 a side / 6 a side (normal cricket rules)

This game is for adults and more able players. 16–20 overs per side. Normal cricket rules apply, except that batsmen retire at 25 or 30 runs, and can bat again if the whole team are bowled out before the overs are completed (optional rule). 16-over match, no bowler can bowl more than four overs. 20-over match, no bowler can bowl more than five overs.

LAYOUT FOR THE GAME

NEVER USE CRICKET BALLS INDOORS

USE CRICKET BALLS OUTDOORS ONLY, AND ONLY WITH COMPETENT PLAYERS

1. Set up game as shown opposite.

2. If indoors, all fielders stand against the wall. If outdoors, they can be in normal fielding positions.

3. Position incoming batsmen behind the wickets ON THE OFF SIDE OF THE HALL IN A CORNER, standing outside playing area when possible — SAFETY.

4. Square leg must stand straighter when playing in a small sports hall. NEVER PUT SMALLER CHILDREN IN THIS POSITION — SAFETY. Change them with a more competent player.

5. Fielders in front of the wicket must be no closer than 11 yards from the batsman — SAFETY.

RULES OF THE GAME

1. Each team starts with a score of 200 runs.

2. Batsmen can be out in the usual ways, and also:
   (a) by hitting the ceiling of the hall
   (b) by being caught off the walls, except when hitting a 6

3. Unlimited lives. If you're out, score –6 off team's score.

4. Scoring runs:
   - Back wall along the ground, score 4
   - Back wall in the air, score 6 (can't be caught off back wall)
   - Side walls, score 2 plus any additional singles that are run
   - Back wall behind the stumps, score 1 plus any additional singles that are run
   - Wides, byes and leg byes, score 1 and an extra ball (be lenient with younger players/beginners)
   - No LBWs

   Coach must always umpire and score.

5. Batsmen bat together in pairs (e.g. four or five overs a pair, depending on time available).

6. Batsmen can be run out at either end.

7. Bowlers bowl six balls per over, always from the same end. Batsmen change ends at the end of an over.

8. Batsmen change ends when a wicket falls.

9. For younger players and beginners, batsmen should face no more than four consecutive balls. Change ends to ensure equal involvement of batsmen.

10. All players including wicket keeper rotate clockwise after each over, unless you have a specialist wicket keeper. For older players, playing a 16-over game, no bowler should bowl more than four overs. Not all fielders need bowl.

11. NOTE — Don't allow fast bowlers to bowl at less able batsmen (switch sequence).

42

PLAYING YOURSELF IN

THIS CHART SHOWS THE LOW-RISK SHOTS TO PLAY WHEN YOU FIRST GO INTO BAT
THINK! CONCENTRATE AND FOCUS ON THE CENTRE OF THE BALL — AND RELAX
REMEMBER — PATIENCE AND DISCIPLINED SHOT SELECTION

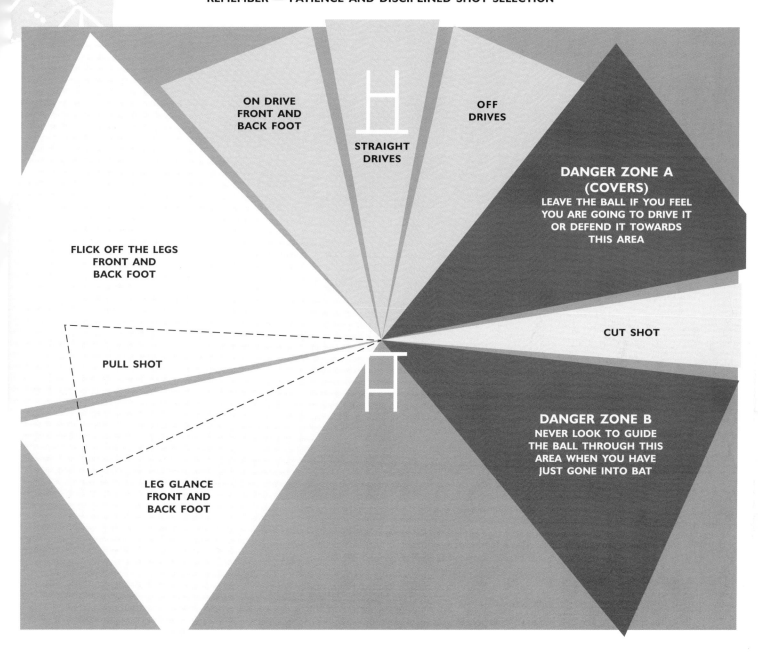

OFF, ON AND STRAIGHT DRIVES

These drives are safe shots to play as the bat is behind the ball for the longest amount of time in relation to the other shots.
If you play with a straight bat and good technique as well as judging the correct length to drive, you will not get out. Early on in
your innings, try to stroke the ball towards these areas. Don't try to hit the ball too hard.

FLICKS OFF THE LEGS

For the good batsman the flick off the legs is a safe shot to play when accumulating runs. The ball is outside the leg stump so you can't get out
bowled or LBW. Just make sure you get your head forward of the body and lean into the shot. Stroke the ball — Don't try to hit it too hard.

THE LEG GLANCES

This is a good safe shot to accumulate runs against a fast bowler with very little risk of getting out. The ball is a good length but is outside
the line of leg stump. You can't be bowled or LBW. Just use the pace of the ball to steer it towards fine leg.

THE CUT SHOT

The cut shot is a good shot to use for early runs on the board. It is useful to put away a bad ball against a fast bowler. If you don't feel confident
enough early in your innings to play the shot just leave it alone. (Don't cut early on in your innings on a wicket with uneven bounce!)

DANGER ZONES A AND B

It is risky to drive or defend a ball towards the danger zones because the ball is wide of the off stump and the bat is not on the line
of the ball for long. You risk being caught behind. Wait until you get your eye in and you are used to the pace and bounce of the pitch,
then start to play the cover drives — but make sure the ball is a half volley and not a length ball.

THE PULL SHOT

The pull shot is a good shot for putting away a bad ball (long hop) bowled by a spin bowler on a wicket with true bounce.
Never try to play a pull shot against a fast bowler, or on a wicket where the ball is keeping low.

QUESTIONS
TO ASK YOURSELF
ABOUT THE PSYCHOLOGICAL SIDE OF BATTING

1. What is concentration?

2. When do you start thinking about your innings?

3. What aspects of the game do you take into consideration before and during your innings?

4. What is your game plan in the following situations, and how will you achieve it?
   (a) 10 overs remaining, 50 to win   (b) 10 overs remaining, 80 to win

5. What is the most important procedure/focus as the bowler starts to run up to bowl?

6. Why is a batsman confident?

7. How do you regain confidence?

Write down a short explanation on each of the above points.

HOW TO SCORE 100

I want to score a century — How do I achieve this?
Just bat away and it will happen? No!
You must have a strategy, a personal game plan

Put the thought of 100 away to the BACK of your mind
Believe you can do it, but set yourself a series of smaller targets

REMEMBER! CONCENTRATION / PATIENCE / DISCIPLINED SHOT SELECTION / CONFIDENCE / BE POSITIVE.
TIP (Relaxed in body alert with mind.)

BEFORE THINKING ABOUT YOUR PLAN, TAKE THE FOLLOWING INTO CONSIDERATION

1. The present game situation.
2. The type of wicket, and its condition.
3. The type of bowler and what type of deliveries he is capable of bowling.
4. The fielders and their positions.
5. Who you are batting with, and how long he has been in.

YOUR GAME PLAN

1. Break down your century into a series of small, realistic targets which are easy to achieve (e.g. a series of 10-run targets).
2. Only play at the balls on the stumps. Leave length balls outside off stump.
3. Score off bad balls and leg side deliveries.
4. Play in a narrow V.
5. Look for quick singles. Don't look to hit boundaries — they will come anyway.
   Stroke the ball with correct technique, and keep the score ticking over (one-day cricket).

HOW TO ACHIEVE THE ABOVE CONSISTENTLY AND SUCCESSFULLY?

1. Focused, relaxed concentration on the centre of the ball.
2. Overall awareness of all of the above.
3. Disciplined shot selection. Contain your eagerness, and be patient.
4. Positive attitude and self-belief: "I can do this".
5. Guts, determination and being hungry for success.

" When I reach 50 I will concentrate even harder —
I won't be impatient and try to hit my way to 100 "

REMEMBER —

Discipline starts off the field: punctuality, dress, practice, etc.

Condition your practice to simulate live match conditions
Practice regularly, with a purpose and in a disciplined manner
Above all, enjoy your cricket!

44

CONCENTRATION

When you get to a high level, 80% of batting is in the mind, 20% is technique. CONCENTRATION is wiping everything out of your mind except the job in hand (e.g. before you face the first ball, focus on the centre of the ball). Remember - relaxed in body, alert in mind

How many times have you been out because you lost concentration? You could have prevented this.

1. Playing at a wide ball
2. Hitting the ball into the air
3. Hitting across the line
4. Trying to score too early in your innings (rushing, and making shots under pressure)
5. Too eager to hit boundaries
6. Getting run out
7. NOT WATCHING THE BALL
8. Overcoming fears

GOOD, FOCUSED CONCENTRATION CAN ELIMINATE ALL OF THESE, MAKING YOU MORE SUCCESSFUL AND MORE CONFIDENT.

What is the game plan?

1. Accumulating runs: 2 or 3 per over.
    How do we do this? Quick singles and good running between the wickets.

2. Pick up the run rate: hitting boundaries.
    How do we do this? Where are my strengths? (Line up the balls.)
    Disciplined shot selection. Strike the ball with correct technique.

What sort of pitch? What sort of bowler?

1. Wet wicket: only hit balls that are really there.
    Punish the bad ball — GET TO THE PITCH.

2. Hard pitch first bowlers favour the back foot.
    USE THE PACE OF THE BALL. Let the ball come.

The batsman's train of thought from the dressing room to the first ball

Focusing on the job in hand (in order of importance, point 4 being the most important):

1. The pitch, the bowlers, the fielders.
2. Game plan: What is my task?
3. Confidence: I can do the job!
4. Finally, focus on the ball, even before the bowler starts his run up.

BATTING THOUGHTS

Set a realistic innings goal. Believe you can achieve it. Successfully visualise achieving it in detail. Focus your mind, concentrate on the ball and do it!

1. **When do you start to think about your innings?**

    Before you get to the middle. When you arrive at the ground. NOT just before facing the first ball!

2. **What things should you consider when thinking about an innings?**

    PITCH — Is it a wet pitch? Slow and low? Hard and bouncing? Turning square, seaming?
    BOWLERS — Fast? Spinners? Medium pacers?
    FIELDERS — Weak fielders? Strong fielders? Fielders standing too deep?
    MATCH SITUATION — Overs remaining? Runs needed? How long to bat out for a draw?

3. **Overall team targets and game plan**

    (a) How many runs do you need (runs per over)? (b) Playing for a draw? (c) Declaration time. How long to bat? What's your target?

4. **What is your individual target and game plan?**

    (a) How many runs per over? (b) Give the strike to the man who is already in. (c) Keep the score ticking over. Think about how — Quick singles. (d) What do you see as your scoring shots?

5. **How are you going to achieve it?**

    For example: (a) Get quick singles, bring the fielders in. (b) Pierce the gaps. (c) Hit bad balls. (d) Patience and good, DISCIPLINED shot selection!

6. **Total self-belief**

    "I can do this, whatever the situation. I am the man for the job, here and how, today."

7. **Finally …**

    CONCENTRATE ON THE BALL (from the bowler's hand) — FOCUS!

NEVER DOUBT YOURSELF

ALWAYS BELIEVE THAT YOU CAN DO THE JOB IN HAND

ALWAYS BE POSITIVE AND BELIEVE YOU CAN WIN!

RUNNING A NET SESSION

SAFETY + MAXIMUM ACTIVITY + TECHNICAL INPUT + PRAISE → IMPROVEMENT

1. SIX PLAYERS PER NET

   One padding up, four bowling, one batting.

   Make sure batting time is shared equally among the players. (Time it with a watch.)

2. FACILITY SAFETY

   (a) Check nets for holes.

   (b) Find out where the nearest phone is (in case of emergency), and check for first aid kit.

   (c) Make sure cricket mats are taped down at the ends.

3. INTRODUCTION

   (a) Introduce yourself. Say your name and, briefly, who you are.

   (b) Ask their names. Ask if the bowlers have any injuries you should know about.

4. NET SAFETY

   (a) Show how to retrieve balls from side of net safely:

   - Batsman — Push bat into side netting, keeping head well away from the net. With your foot, roll ball into middle of practice area. Pick it up a safe distance from the net.
   - Bowler — Retrieve ball with your foot, keeping head well away from the net. Look out for anyone batting in the next door net. Pick it up a safe distance from the net.

   (b) Explain to bowler to always watch the batsman: BOWLERS MUST NEVER TAKE THEIR EYES OFF THE BATSMAN, ESPECIALLY WHEN WALKING BACK TO THE MARK.

   (c) When to bowl — Don't bowl until previous bowler has walked back past the stumps you are going to bowl from.

   (d) Make sure the batsman is fully kitted out.

   ASK IF HE IS WEARING A BOX. If he is not HE MUST NOT BAT, unless using a soft ball (e.g. an Incrediball®).

   He should:

   - Wear a helmet if he has one.
   - Wear a thigh pad inside trousers.
   - If possible, take off all jewellery and watches.

   You should:

   - Give batsman a guard, from directly behind the stumps at the bowler's end, where you will be.
   - Where possible, he should mark his guard with chalk (provided by you) behind the stumps at the batsman's end.

5. THE COACH

   (a) Should be well turned out, in whites.

   (b) Should always have his bat with him, for demonstrations. (Place bat at back of net in side netting when not in use.)

6. COACHING IN THE NET

   If you feel the need to go down the net to explain a fault to a batsman:

   (a) Take all the balls off the bowlers. Make sure they are at the back of the net, watching the batsman.

   (b) Batsman demonstrates his shot. Coach shows the correct shot. Batsman copies coach.

   (c) Coach then gives batsman a few feeds. Finish on a good shot.

   Allow five minutes maximum for this procedure.

7. BOWLER TO BATSMAN COACHING RATIOS

   Give as much coaching to batsmen as to bowlers.

   For the first few minutes of a batsman's innings watch him and weigh up his ability, allowing him to settle in before you begin to coach him. Similarly, let each bowler bowl for a few minutes before you attempt to correct any faults.

8. SET UP THE BOWLING

   (a) Get the bowlers to mark out their run-ups (using chalk).

   (b) Check their grips, but don't change anything at this stage. Observe players' ability first. (See also point 11.)

   (c) Give a bowling order.

9. SET REALISTIC TARGETS

   For example, 4 balls left, 8 runs to win; or 4 balls, don't get out.

10. SUMMARY OF NET SESSION AS A GROUP

    Batsman – Begin by praising him, then recap on coaching points. Bowlers to listen as well.

    Bowlers – Again, begin with praise. For each bowler, recap points needing work. Other bowlers to listen.

    Close the session with general encouragement and arrange to see them again.

11. NOTE — BE FLEXIBLE!

    If a batsman or bowler is playing successfully, but in an unorthodox way, don't be too hasty to make him change.

    If something is working well, leave it.

FAULTS AND FAULT ANALYSIS

FAULTS

FAULT ANALYSIS

BOWLED AND LBW
(Hitting across the line)

IN GENERAL
• Picking bat up towards gully too much.
• Picking bat up behind leg stump.
• Opening leading shoulder too early in shot.
• Turning leading shoulder too much so that you become too far sideways on or too open.
• Too much bottom hand during backlift.
• Eyes not level, so tipping towards the off side and getting stuck on the crease.
• Collapsing leading elbow during straight-batted shots.

FRONT FOOT
• When going forward you put your front foot too far sideways, bending your front knee.
  This causes you to take too small a stride and also to walk out of your crease off balance.

BACK FOOT
• Not getting eyes and head into line and going back and across to cover your stumps (leg and middle).
• Back foot not parallel to the crease, so body position is square on. This causes hitting across the line.

CAUGHT IN THE
SLIPS OR GULLY AREA

IN GENERAL
• Picking bat up behind the leg stump or too far outside off stump.
• Playing at balls too far wide of the off stump.
• Trying to hit straight balls too square of the wicket on the off side.

FRONT FOOT
• Not putting your foot to the ball.

BACK FOOT
• Not getting back and across in line with the ball.
• Falling away as you play the shot.
• Collapsing elbow too early during the shot.

CAUGHT ON THE LEG SIDE

• Head too far over towards the off side in the stance. (Feet too close together.)
• Putting foot straight across the crease and leaning towards the off side.
• Eyes not level, so head tips to the off side and body tips over.
• Head not forward of the body, so leaning back and not over the ball.

FRONT FOOT ONLY
• Too big a stride down the wicket, so head is not forward of the body. (Leaning back.)
• Collapsing back leg because of the above.

CAUGHT IN THE V OR
COVERS AREA

• Trying to hit a drive to a good length ball. (Not there to drive.)
• Not letting the ball come and being drawn to play the shot too early. Relax and let it come.

CAUGHT SQUARE COVER
• Putting your foot straight up the wicket and hitting the ball behind your front foot, so leaning back and using bottom hand too much.

CAUGHT AT SHORT LEG
OR SILLY POINT

AGAINST FAST BOWLER
SILLY POINT
• Leaning back too much and trying to hit the ball too early. Relax and let it come.
SHORT LEG
• Body position over towards the off side too much.
• Getting too far sideways on to the leg side delivery.
• Not going back and across behind the line of the ball.

AGAINST A SPINNER
SILLY POINT
• Playing against the spin.
• Playing the ball too early.
• Position too chest on.
• Pushing at the ball too hard.
• Playing the ball behind your pad.
SHORT LEG
• Playing against the spin.
• Playing the ball too early.
• Position too sideways on.
• Pushing at the ball too hard.
• Playing the ball behind your pad.

HIT ON THE HEAD

• Not getting back and across the crease (i.e. backing away).
• Taking your eye off the ball.

RELATE THESE FAULTS TO THE PICTURE CARDS OF SHOTS AS THEY SHOULD BE PLAYED!

The Cricket CoachMaster

INGREDIENTS FOR SUCCESS

ALL GREAT PLAYERS POSSESS THESE QUALITIES ...

1. ENJOYMENT

   You must enjoy playing to perform well.

2. 100% WORK RATE

   You must practise regularly and give 100%.
   Practise good habits, not bad ones.

3. TOTAL FOCUS

   You must be totally focused, both in practice and in matches.
   Always make your practice specific and constructive.
   Practise your powers of concentration.

4. DISCIPLINE

   You must be disciplined in your practice so you can be disciplined in matches.

5. SELF-BELIEF

   You must believe that you can do the job, both with the bat and with the ball, and
   have the confidence that you can perform well, meeting *realistic* targets.
   Remember – Strive for *calculated confidence, not mindless arrogance*!

6. CONSISTENCY

   Aim for consistency, both in practice and in matches. Consistency leads to success.

7. TECHNIQUE

   You must work to achieve good technique, in batting and bowling.
   Keep working on your technique, to maintain and improve it.

8. GOAL SETTING

   Always set personal goals, in practice and in matches.
   Your goals should always be:
   S   Specific
   M   Measurable
   A   Achievable
   R   Realistic
   T   Timely

9. PROFESSIONALISM

   You need to be dedicated to your sport, in appearance, attitude and performance.

10. DETERMINATION

    You must be determined in practice, and hungry for success in matches.
    If you want it enough, you *will* achieve it.

11. FITNESS

    You must condition your body wih regular training.
    The fitter you are, the longer you can concentrate and the better you will
    perform under pressure.

**IF YOU LACK IN ANY OF THESE AREAS,
YOU ARE NOT GIVING YOURSELF THE BEST CHANCE OF SUCCESS.**

PINPOINT YOUR WEAKER AREAS AND WORK HARD TO IMPROVE THEM.

IRON OUT THE FLAWS AND YOU WILL BE ON THE ROAD TO SUCCESS.

**IF YOU WANT TO BE BETTER THAN THE NEXT PLAYER, BE MORE FOCUSED THAN HIM,
TRAIN HARDER AND BELIEVE IN YOURSELF MORE THAN HE DOES.**

Cricket must be counted amongst the most technical and **unnatural** of games. A blacksmith's bumper and a farmer's swipe may occasionally succeed but such rudimentary skills seldom reach the greater stages upon which this difficult game is played. Only with diligent practice of the correct techniques can mastery be achieved. It is of particular importance that the right approach is encouraged in young practitioners or error swiftly applies its vice-like grip and another ambitious youth will be condemned to a life of edging to slip deliveries which, with better instruction, might otherwise have been driven satisfyingly to the boundary.

It is in the interests of solving the game's mysteries and promoting proper batting techniques that Gary Palmer has produced this illuminating manual. A lively cricketer himself and a coach rich in experience, Mr Palmer has studied the game in detail and this manual will help players old and young to understand and improve their game.

Nor is this manual merely instructional. Mr Palmer is an innovative man and here he outlines various entertaining games within a game, all of them calculated to stimulate and inform youthful interests. This manual can be warmly recommended to any aspiring players and any coach eager to rejuvenate himself and the youngsters in his charge.

Peter Roebuck
Cricket Writer of the Sunday Telegraph
Sidney Morning Herald
Captain of Somerset 1986-88

The coaching manual is very thorough and detailed accounts on how to play and coach the various batting shots. All the photographs of the strokes are very clear and give a step by step text which will teach even a county cricketer to understand the techniques of better batting, as well as highlighting his possible faults.

The manual will give safe, organised, efficient ways of practising the shots in group coaching situations. The games section has some very novel ideas for enjoyable conditioned games which highlight cricket awareness. University PE coaches and players learning to coach or about to take coaching awards in cricket would find this manual useful to study from.

The batting section will make the teacher, the coach or professional cricketer a better player and a more versatile coach with a greater understanding of batting techniques.

I have a manual and recommend you buy one.

Graeme Hick
Worcester and England cricketer

I am writing with regard to the informative coach book produced by Gary Palmer. It is packed full of information and the photography and accompanying text is clear and well structured. Not only would the information gathered be useful to players seeking to improve their own game, but also would be extremely useful from a coaching point of view.

Unfortunately the product wasn't available when I was learning the game, but hopefully it will be widely available to the young cricketers of the future.

Peter Such
Essex and England cricketer

This is one of the best coaching manuals I have seen because it is so comprehensive and clear. It is essential reading for every cricket coach and player who wants to improve their playing and coaching abilities.

Gary Palmer is technically one of the best young coaches I have met. His attention to detail is very thorough. He is quick to spot faults and has the ability to correct them with his innovative ideas. I would not hesitate to ask him for advice if I was having problems with my own game. This manual has been particularly useful for me when I have had to group coach children.

If all batsmen have a booklet, it would make my job as a bowler more difficult.

Andy Caddick
Somerset and England cricketer

This manual in it's early stages has created an interest amongst the following players

John Wright
NEW ZEALAND & KENT COACH

Robin Smith
ENGLAND & HAMPSHIRE

Jimmy Adams
WEST INDIES

Graham Pollock (SOUTH AFRICA)
Gary Palmer (AUTHOR),
Mike Proctor (SOUTH AFRICA & FORMER SA COACH)

Geoff Marsh
Coach of AUSTRALIA (World Cup Winners 1999)

Dean Headley
ENGLAND & KENT